Garbage

Investigate What Happens When You Throw It Out

with 25 Projects

DONNA LATHAM
Illustrated by Beth Hetland

Nomad Press
A division of Nomad Communications
10 9 8 7 6 5 4 3

ISBN Softcover: 978-1-93631-346-4
ISBN Hardcover: 978-1-93631-347-1

Educational Consultant, Marla Conn

Questions regarding the ordering of this book should be addressed to
Nomad Press
2456 Christian St.
White River Junction, VT 05001
www.nomadpress.net

More **Environmental Science** titles from Nomad Press

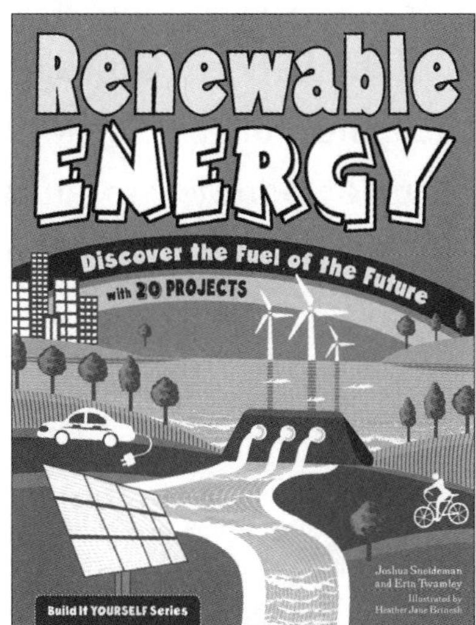

Check out more titles at www.nomadpress.net

Dedication

In loving memory of my grandparents,
Rosa and Carmelo Cilia, champions of stewardship.

Sincere thanks to environmental scientist and first reader Nick Longo; Mary Eileen Sullivan at Friends of the Parks in Chicago; Frances Canonizado at the Alliance for the Great Lakes in Chicago; and rubbish warrior Bonnie Moran at St. John's Episcopal Church Ecology Group in Oakland.

Contents

A Throwaway World

What have you tossed in the garbage today? A gnawed apple core? A squashed juice box? Maybe you threw away a tattered backpack or an old pair of sneakers.

Trash is the stuff we consider useless. Another word for it is garbage. It's what we throw away. Anywhere you find people, you'll find trash—mounds and mounds of it. Garbage is even on the surface of the moon and in the middle of the ocean.

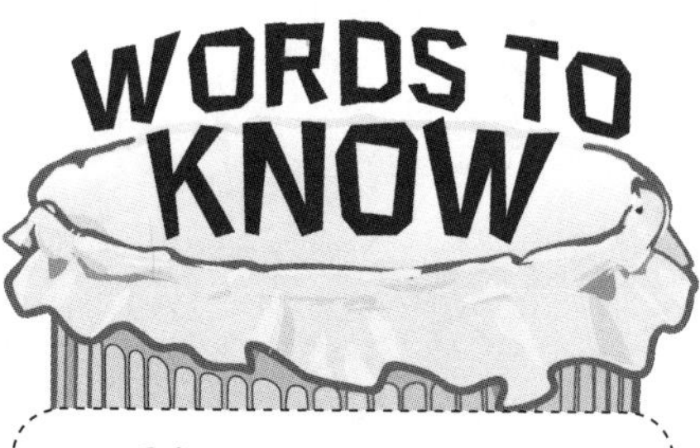

landfill: a huge area of land where trash gets buried.

incinerator: a large furnace that burns trash.

environment: everything in nature, living and nonliving, including animals, plants, rocks, soil, and water.

We don't realize how much stuff we throw away. In just one year, an average family in the United States churns out 6,600 pounds of waste (2,994 kilograms). That's enough to fill a three-bedroom house to the ceiling. And trash doesn't always make it to a garbage can. It's often left behind as messy litter that people carelessly scatter. Litter flutters across our streets, parks, and beaches. No wonder so many people are talking trash these days!

Trash gets jam-packed into **landfills** or burned in **incinerators**. In her book, *Gone Tomorrow: The Hidden Life of Garbage*, Heather Rogers writes that most people haul loaded garbage cans to the curb at night and take in empty ones in the morning. Trash is out of sight, out of mind. And we're happy not to see our garbage or catch a whiff of it again.

Trash Flash

Garbage is out of this world! During the historic 1969 *Apollo 11* mission, astronauts Neil Armstrong and Buzz Aldrin gathered rocks and soil on the moon. The astronauts left behind their boot prints and an American flag. And a heap of space trash. To lighten the *Apollo's* load and make room to transport samples back to Earth, the astronauts left empty food sacks, vomit bags, a TV camera, collection tongs, and magazines on the moon. They even left the space boots that made the famous footprints.

But what happens to all that garbage once it leaves our hands?

Like many people, you probably care about keeping the **environment** clean and healthy. In a world crowded with almost 7 billion people, it's easy to think one person can't make a difference. But you can. Every effort counts. Become a rubbish warrior like some of the people you'll meet in this book.

Rubbish Warriors

On your mark, get set, go! Trash running is a sporty new craze that's sweeping the country. In places like Portland, Maine, and Chicago, Illinois, Trash Runners zip through woody trails, across beaches, or on city streets grabbing litter. It's a win-win situation. The runners get a fantastic workout and the environment gets cleaned up!

TRY IT!

Start your own Trash Runners group. Organize friends and family to run with you. Everyone totes a collection bag and trots through a target area. The trick is to snatch litter without breaking stride. Talk about grab and go! To see how others are doing it, go to www.atayne.com/impact/trash-runners.

The Four Rs: Reduce, Reuse, Recycle, Rethink

In this book you'll explore ways you can **reduce**, **reuse**, and **recycle** garbage. You'll also find ways to **rethink** the choices you make every day. To reduce is to use less of a product or material so there's less waste. For example, instead of grabbing three paper towels to dry your hands after washing up, use one.

reduce: to use less of something.

reuse: instead of tossing out an item, using it again or for a new or creative purpose.

recycle: shredding, squashing, pulping, or melting items to use the materials to create new products.

rethink: to reconsider—to think about something again and change your mind about it.

resource: things found in nature. such as wood or gold, that people can use.

scavenge: to find usable bits and parts from discarded stuff.

To reuse is to save things that you would normally throw out—and use them again, or for another purpose. Turn an old beach towel into a cozy blanket for your pet. Pass along clothes to family or friends, or donate books to a library.

To recycle means to break down old items in order to make new ones. Recycling saves **resources** and energy. Some materials that are commonly recycled include plastic, paper, glass, and metal.

What's rethinking? It's looking more closely at something and thinking again about your choices. By rethinking your habits, you might change them for the better. For example, do you drink bottled water at soccer practice or dance rehearsal?

JUST For Fun!

What's a great example of a collective noun?

Garbage can.

Did you know that it requires 1.5 million barrels of oil to produce a year's worth of bottled water? That's enough fuel for 100,000 cars for a year. After rethinking, you might decide to fill up a reusable stainless steel water bottle instead.

What has your pencil been before? Old money and blue jeans get recycled into pencils.

In our throwaway world, we toss out trash constantly. But what does "out" really mean? And where, exactly, is away? What happens when we run out of out and away? Trash may be out of sight. But try to keep it in mind.

About the Projects

Use the projects and activities in this book to make your own discoveries about garbage and to spark new ideas about how to tackle waste. Don't have all the materials and supplies needed for a project? Think of items you can substitute. **Scavenge** stuff from a friend, or trade with someone. Of course, safety's first, so ask adults for help when handling sharp items and glue guns or when using the stove.

Trash Flash

There are lots of words to describe the things we throw out. What does debris mean to you? You might imagine demolished walls left after a tornado whirls through a neighborhood. How about leftovers? They could be the uneaten food from last night's meal. What do the following terms for trash make you think of?

bits and pieces	discards	litter	rubbish
cast-offs	garbage	odds and ends	scraps
debris	junk	refuse	surplus
	leftovers	rejects	waste

How Much Garbage Do You Produce?

Families throw out old laptops, avocado pits, blobs of burritos, chicken bones, and cordless phones. Folks dump ratty sweaters and raggedy blue jeans. We discard piles and piles of disposable products like diapers, napkins, and paper towels.

Garbage is an unavoidable part of our lives. But in our throwaway world we've racked up some mind-boggling **statistics**.

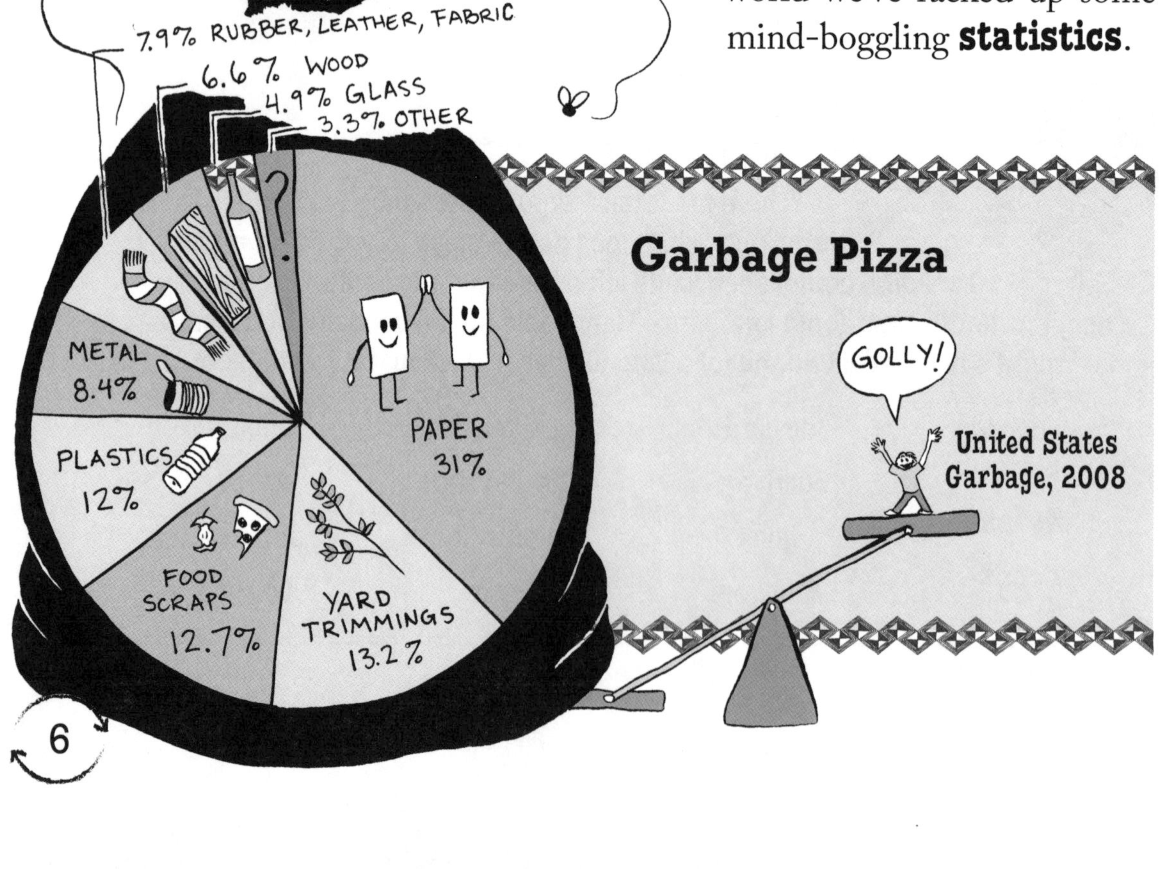

Garbage Pizza

United States Garbage, 2008

GOLLY!

PAPER 31%
YARD TRIMMINGS 13.2%
FOOD SCRAPS 12.7%
PLASTICS 12%
METAL 8.4%
7.9% RUBBER, LEATHER, FABRIC
6.6% WOOD
4.9% GLASS
3.3% OTHER

The United States alone generates a whopping 260 million tons of garbage a year (236 million metric tons). That's enough trash to cover the state of Texas—twice.

From this gigantic amount, let's zoom in on just one person. You. If you're like the average American, then you produce about 4½ pounds of rubbish a day (2 kilograms), over 31 pounds a week (14 kilograms). That's 1,638 pounds of trash a year (743 kilograms)!

What's rotting in those mounds of rubbish? It's all just gross and repulsive junk, right? Not exactly. In 2008, the **Environmental Protection Agency** collected **data** about the kinds of refuse America produces. How do you think your own garbage measures up?

Kinds of Waste

Most of the waste shown in the Garbage Pizza does not need to go in the landfill. The paper, plastic, metal, and glass can be recycled. What about the food scraps and yard trimmings? **Compost** them! Food scraps and yard waste **decay** in the compost pile, turning into **nutrient**-rich soil to put back into the earth.

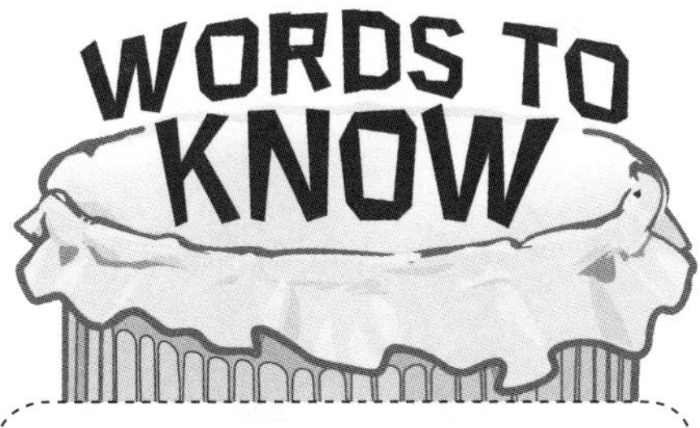

disposable: made to be thrown away after using once.

statistics: numbers that show facts about a subject.

Environmental Protection Agency (EPA): a department of the government concerned with the environment and its impact on human health.

data: information, facts, and numbers.

compost: decayed food scraps and vegetation that can be put back in the soil.

decay: to rot.

nutrients: the substances in food and soil that keep animals and plants healthy and growing.

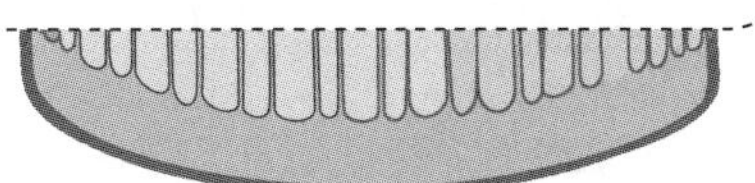

Every hour of the day, Americans throw away 2.5 million plastic bottles.

organic: something that is or was living, such as wood, paper, grass, and insects.

inorganic: not part of the living world, such as tin and glass.

biodegradable: able to decay and break down.

decomposers: bacteria, insects, and fungi that break down plant and animal wastes and cause them to decay.

fungi: mold, mildew, rust, and mushrooms. Plural of fungus.

Trash contains both **organic** and **inorganic** waste. Organic waste consists of plant and animal material. They are part of nature and were once alive, such as yard trimmings or food scraps. Organic waste is **biodegradable** and can be composted. It decays quickly with the help of **decomposers**.

Decomposers are tiny, living recyclers such as bacteria, **fungi**, slugs, and worms. They feast on decaying plant and animal material, breaking them down into nutrients that are absorbed by the soil. These nutrients then become food for new plants and animals, and the circle of life continues.

TRY IT!

Look at this list of items many families might throw away. Decide if each is organic or inorganic waste.

- coffee grounds
- newspapers
- lettuce and tomato scraps
- hamburger buns
- batteries
- dryer lint
- plastic grocery bags
- scrap paper
- old magazines
- empty vitamin bottles
- empty tubes of toothpaste
- tubes from paper towels and toilet paper
- tea bags
- egg shells
- carrot and cucumber peels
- fabric softener sheets
- empty containers of laundry detergent

That's why organic waste has a **closed-loop life cycle**, which means it never actually ends.

Inorganic waste is not made from plants or animals. It doesn't break down quickly. Inorganic waste includes glass, plastics, and metals. Inorganic waste has a **linear life cycle**. When we throw it away, its life cycle ends. Do you think your garbage contains more organic or inorganic waste?

WORDS TO KNOW

closed-loop life cycle: the life cycle for organic material that never comes to an end.

linear life cycle: the life cycle for inorganic material that comes to an end when it is thrown away.

Trash Flash

Pewww! What makes that funky odor wafting from your trash? It's organic waste, such as festering fruits and veggies, putrid meats, and fish. As food scraps decay, they stink up garbage with a smell like rotten eggs. Most inorganic waste doesn't smell when you throw it away.

Ocean Garbage

Swirling in the Pacific Ocean between California and Hawaii is an enormous blob twice the size of the state of Texas. What in the world is it? It's a floating trash dump known as the Great Pacific Garbage Patch.

What did the eyes say to the nose?

Just between us, something smells.

Experts estimate that the Garbage Patch contains more than 3.5 million tons of rubbish (3.2 million metric tons). Mostly made of plastic, the drifting dump threatens animal life. Dolphins, seals, and seabirds choke on plastic pellets and die. People are affected, too. Fish eat plants in these polluted waters, and then people eat the fish.

Rubbish Warriors

"If a lot of people come together and do little things," Chad Pregracke said in a *CBS News* interview, "it adds up to big things." He should know.

Chad grew up along the Mississippi River. As a student, he camped on islands that dot the river. Tired of sleeping out on trash-strewn shorelines, Chad decided to clean up the river "one piece of garbage at a time."

In 1998, he launched a clean-up organization called Living Lands and Waters. The group travels in barges along many of the nation's major rivers picking up rubbish.

So far, 60,000 volunteers have lent a helping hand. Since Living Lands and Waters started, more than 6 million pounds of river junk has been cleared away (3 million kilograms)!

Trash Flash

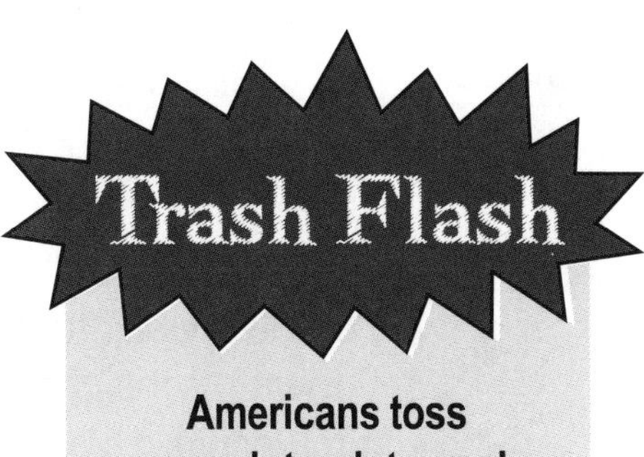

Americans toss enough trash to pack 63,000 garbage trucks. Every day!

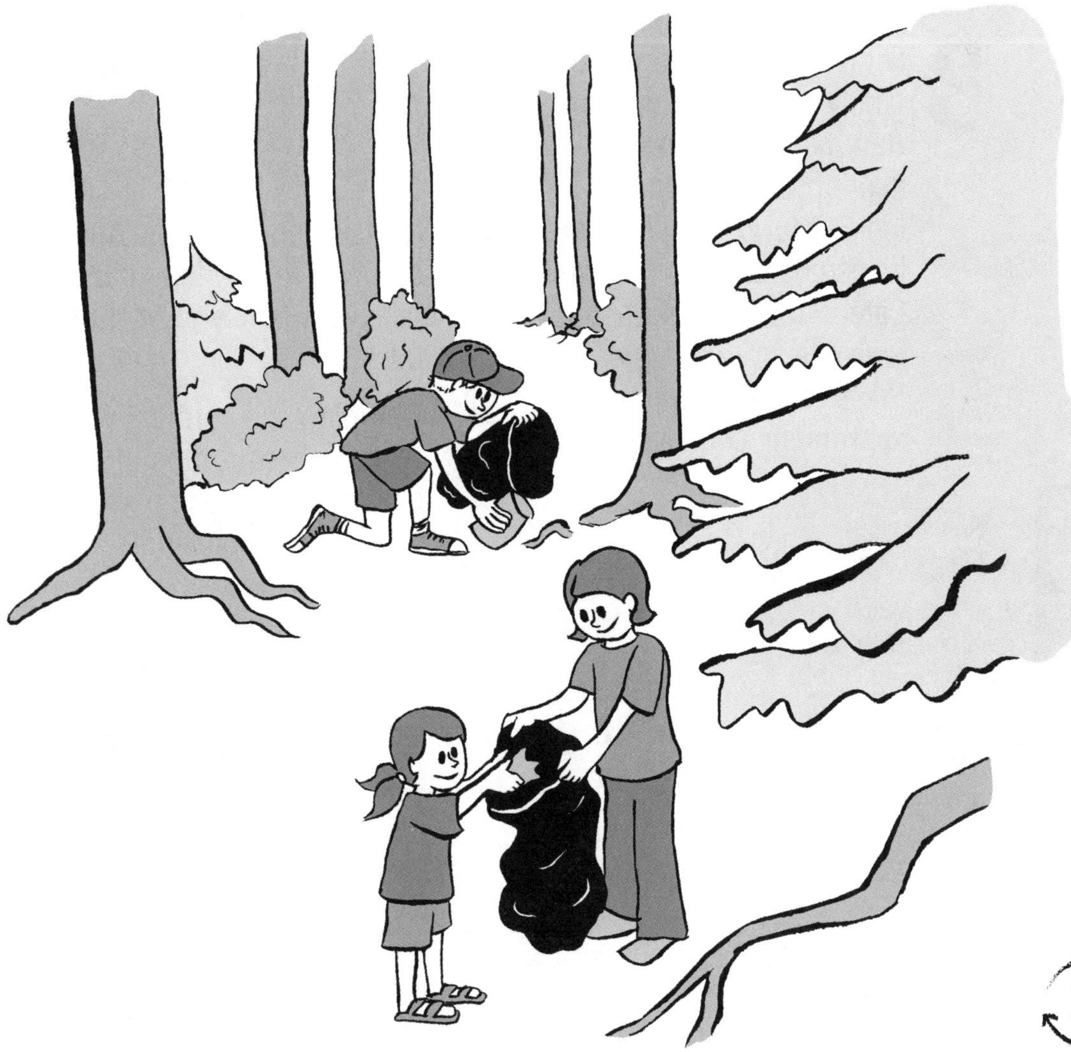

Track Your Trash

What's in your rubbish? For one week, track and record every item your family discards. Be very careful because trash can contain broken or sharp things.

1. Use the scale to weigh the empty plastic tubs. Jot down the weights on scratch paper.
2. Reuse cardboard, index cards, or scratch paper to make three labels for the tubs: Trash, Reusable, Recyclable. Tape the labels to the tubs.
3. For one week, become your family's garbage collector. Rummage through every item of trash. Be on the lookout for broken or sharp items and handle with care. Categorize each as trash, reusable, or recyclable. Place each article in the appropriate container.

4. At the end of the week, weigh each tub of stuff. Subtract the original weight of the empty tub from the total, and record how much waste each tub has.
5. Review your findings. Any surprises? How long did it take your family to fill three tubs?
6. Compare and contrast your totals with those the EPA collected. Did each person in your household produce about 31½ pounds of garbage (14 kilograms)? Are you above or below the national average?

SUPPLIES

- scale
- 3 large plastic tubs
- scratch paper, cardboard, or index cards
- permanent markers
- masking tape
- your household trash

TRY IT!

Finished sorting and categorizing your garbage? Generate your own pie graph to illustrate your results. Visit http://nces.ed.gov/nceskids/createagraph/.

7 Challenge your family to cut down your amount of garbage. How can you rethink your trash choices? What can you reuse or recycle, instead of discarding? If you get a composter, you can compost your food waste.

8 A month from now, try this activity again to observe your success.

According to the United Nations, 1 billion people across the world will go to bed hungry tonight. Yet, each year in the United States, people throw out 96 billion pounds of food waste (44 billion kilograms).

Why did the trashcan flunk out of school?

Because his report card was nothing but rubbish.

ACTIVITY

CHAPTER 2

Heaps of History

Throughout human history, people have dumped heaps of rubbish. To archaeologists, ancient discarded garbage isn't junk. It's treasure!

The random odds and ends that people threw away long ago are now considered **artifacts**. They reveal amazing insights about how people used to live and are just as valuable as dazzling jewels. That's why **middens**, which are ancient garbage dumps, are prime places for archaeologists to dig.

Prehistoric People on the Move

Our ancestors were hunter-gatherers. They were **nomadic** people, moving from place to place with the seasons. Several families banded together in small groups and moved from one area to another to find food and fresh water sources.

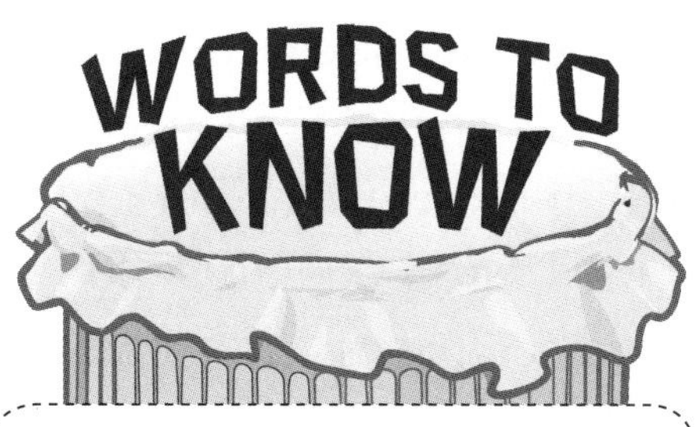

archaeologists: a scientist who studies past human life.

artifact: an object made by people from past cultures, including tools, pottery, and jewelry.

midden: an ancient garbage heap.

nomadic: moving from place to place to find food.

Imagine you're a hunter-gatherer. What does your family do with its garbage? Pile it in a cave to decay? With frequent moves, your family doesn't have enough time to produce heaps and heaps of waste. Sure, there's ash from fires and leftover bones from meals. But this trash is organic. It will decay over time, returning nutrients to the soil. It's a closed-loop life cycle, which is healthy for the planet.

Over the next 5,000 years, however, larger groups of people settled down in one place and started farming. That's when the trash troubles kicked in. Folks needed to figure out where to leave all their garbage.

Trash Flash

When archaeologists explored a prehistoric cave in Spain, they found 13,000-year-old animal bones. From these artifacts, scientists figured out that the cave was a garbage dump where people left animals to decompose after they ate the meat.

Ancient Civilizations Settling Down

Eventually, large groups of people settled in thriving cities. Naturally, these bigger groups produced more garbage. Tons more.

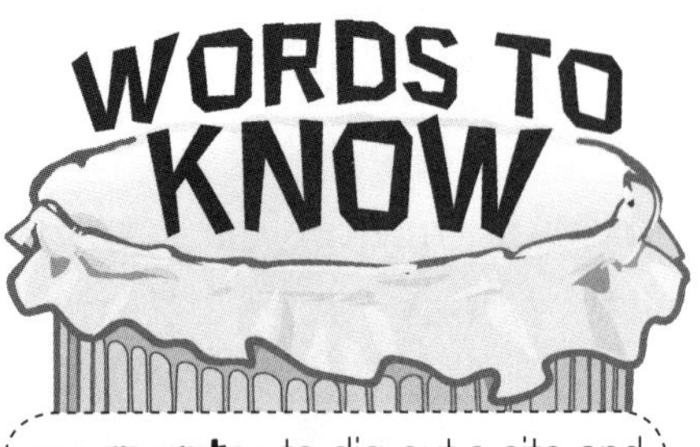

excavate: to dig out a site and its artifacts for study.

garbologist: an archaeologist who studies garbage.

There was no garbage collection back then. So people simply dumped their trash right on the floors of their homes. How do we know? Because archaeologists **excavated** houses at the ancient city of Troy, located in present-day Turkey. People lived in Troy 3,000 to 4,000 years ago. Archaeologists unearthed layers of animal bones left from meals munched long ago.

If you lived during that time, you'd finish eating and just drop your gnawed bones onto the clay floor. What happened when the floors got slimy and rancid? Your family slathered the floor with a fresh layer of earth and clay. Then you piled on more garbage, squashed it underfoot until it got too revolting, and repeated the process. Over and over.

Sometimes all the rubbish didn't fit on the cramped floors. Then it was time to throw it out of the house. People chucked larger chunks of stuff straight out their doors or windows and right into the streets. Wandering pigs, famished cats, and packs of dogs waded through slippery gunk to devour rotting leftovers.

Some archaeologists are garbologists. They dig through landfills to study the garbage a society produced, especially household waste.

When too much trash blocked the streets, it was time to burn it, bury it, or haul it off to putrid dumps on the outskirts of villages. People also threw their garbage into lakes, rivers, and oceans. Good riddance to bad rubbish. Or so they thought.

Trash Flash

Raise the roof! In Troy, people piled so many layers of garbage on their floors that they eventually had to make their roofs higher. It didn't stop there. As the mountains of rubbish rose higher and higher, so did the entire city. New buildings sprang up on top of trash heaps.

People didn't realize the impact their behavior had on one another and on the environment. Their actions caused horrible smells and polluted water supplies. They created ideal conditions for deadly diseases to spread.

Europe in the Middle Ages

During the Middle Ages 1,000 years ago, city populations boomed in Europe. So did garbage and filthy conditions. Unfortunately, people didn't realize there was a link between filth and public health. Streets were like open toilets, where people flung human waste from **chamber pots**. In disgustingly dirty cities, human and animal waste mixed with horse droppings and bloody guts that **slaughterhouses** dumped in the streets.

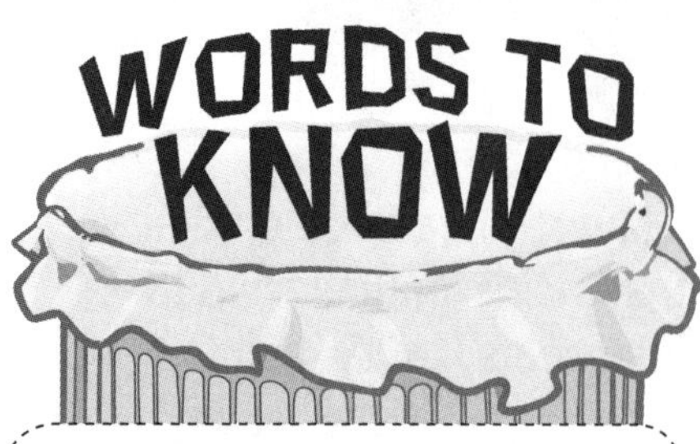

chamber pot: a jug or bowl stashed under beds as a personal port-a-potty.

slaughterhouse: a place where animals are killed for food.

toxic: poisonous.

vermin: small animals or insects that are pests, like cockroaches or mice.

epidemic: a disease that hits large groups at the same time and spreads quickly.

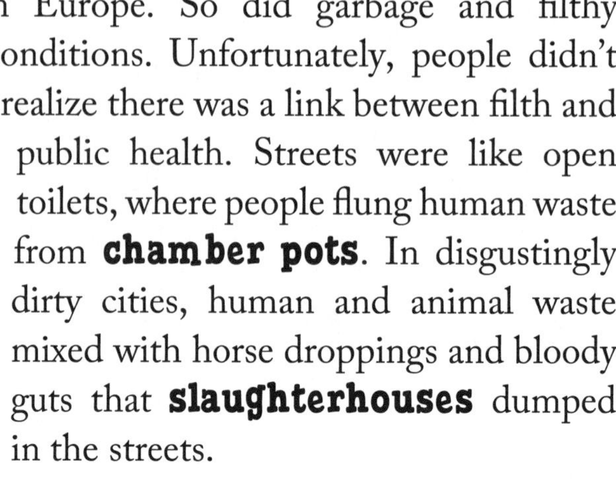

People burned trash, heaped it into giant mounds, or plopped it into the water. Or they just walked around the garbage and tried to ignore the awful smell.

In this **toxic** environment, rats and **vermin** thrived. Fleas carried a deadly disease called the Bubonic Plague. In the mid-1400s, rats carried infected fleas throughout the cities and villages of Europe. The fleas would hop off the rats and onto people, biting them and infecting them with the Plague.

Do tell! Ancient cities in the Middle East rose on top of human-made hills called tells. Heaps of garbage and artifacts, including coins and ceramics, are buried inside tells.

In this way, the Plague galloped through the streets like a racehorse. Called the Black Death because it caused black spots on the skin, it was one of the most devastating **epidemics** in history. The Black Death wiped out nearly 60 percent of Europe's population between 1348 and 1350. It killed a total of 75 million people worldwide.

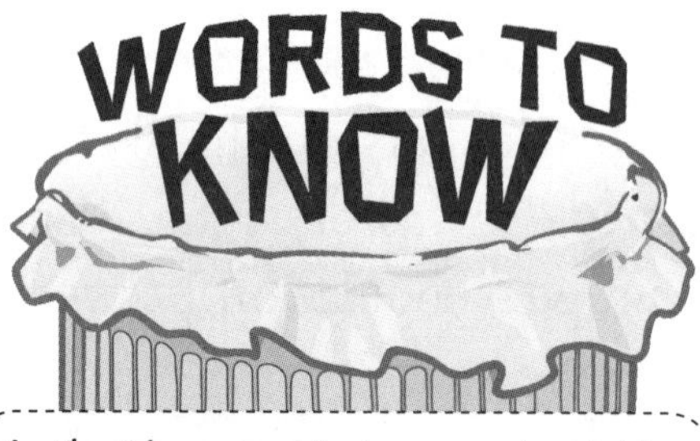

infectious: able to spread quickly from one person to others.

possessions: things you own.

manufactured: made by machines.

thrift: using money carefully.

delirious: restlessness, confusion, and excitement brought on by a high fever, often with mixed-up speech.

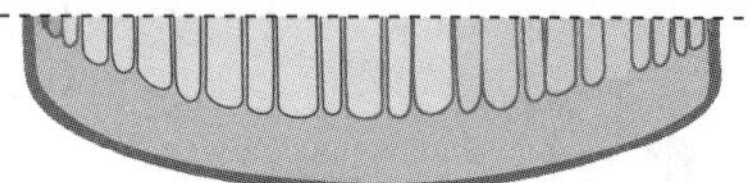

Microscopes hadn't been invented yet, so doctors had no idea what caused the **infectious** disease. Some insisted it was the evil eye. Or mysterious vapors wafting from the planets. Or bad air. Fearing for their own lives, doctors stopped treating the sick. Abandoned by sick owners, dogs, chickens, sheep, and oxen died too. In time, the grisly plague ran its course. One good thing came from the Black Death. People began making a connection between filthy garbage and the spread of disease.

The New World: Waste Not, Want Not

When settlers first arrived in America, they had few **possessions**. Any **manufactured** goods were expensive. People valued **thrift**. They pinched pennies, spent money carefully, and didn't waste what they bought. What they did have was precious to them. What happened to chipped cups and saucers? They weren't thrown away. Instead, folks painstakingly patched them with egg whites, glue, or clay.

Benjamin Franklin was an author, politician, inventor, scientist, and diplomat. In 1757 he was also responsible for launching America's first street-cleaning service in Philadelphia, Pennsylvania.

Trash Flash

It wasn't only Europe in the Middle Ages where garbage caused serious disease. It happened in the United States in Philadelphia, Pennsylvania, in 1793, too. At that time, the bustling port city of Philadelphia was the nation's capital. "Sinks," or open sewers, flowed through unpaved streets. On this trail of guck, a deadly yellow fever epidemic spread through the city during a broiling hot summer. Yellow fever began in Africa and traveled to other parts of the world through the slave trade. Symptoms were horrible. Victims' bones rattled with violent shakes. After a few days, their eyeballs and skin turned yellow. Their noses and gums bled. They vomited black blood. **Delirious** with a raging fever, they babbled nonsense for hours. After a few miserable days, they died.

As with the Black Death, doctors didn't know what caused yellow fever. They didn't realize infectious mosquitoes that thrived in the city's swamps and sinks were the source. After a three-month rampage, the epidemic stopped when cold weather killed the mosquitoes. People finally made a connection between filth and disease and improved sanitation. In 1799, America's first clean-water system launched in Philadelphia.

Pig out! In early America, pigs enjoyed jobs as living garbage disposals. Settlers fed them slops, a mushy mixture of leftover food and kitchen debris. Some towns depended on pigs to get rid of practically all their garbage! Did you know a drove, or group, of pigs can devour a ton of trash a day?

Settlers used food items creatively. After cooking beef and chicken, people stashed leftover animal fat in grease jars. When they had enough, they used it to make soap. Beets and onions bubbling in supper pots produced delicious soup as well as bright dyes for clothing. And after brewing a kettle of evening tea, settlers scooped out the tea leaves to reuse in the next day's pot. When the taste was all boiled away, they dried the leaves and scattered them on the floor to soak up dust.

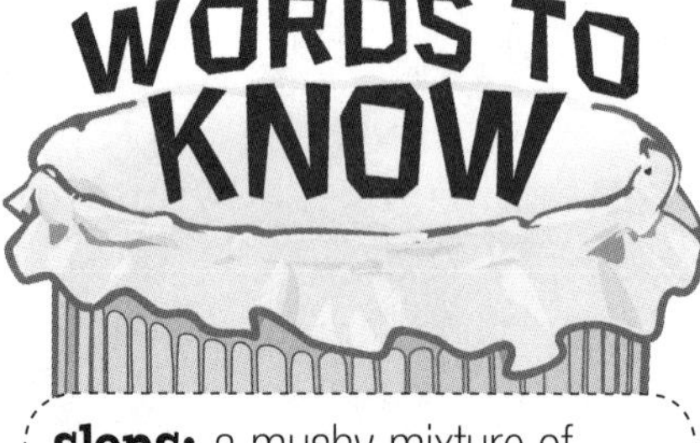

slops: a mushy mixture of kitchen scraps and liquid fed to pigs.

resourceful: able to think of creative solutions to problems.

salvaged: recovered parts or materials that were recycled or reused.

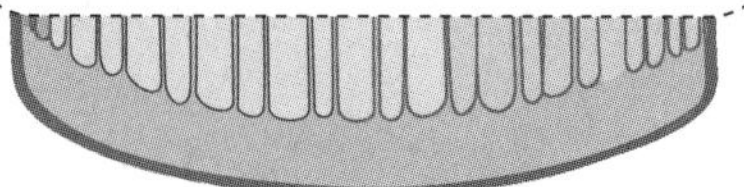

Only the wealthy could afford changes of clothing. Fabric was expensive, so people had to be **resourceful**. Most people had only one or two sets of clothes. Sewing was an important skill that girls learned at a young age. Women mended dresses over and over again with **salvaged** pieces of mismatched fabrics. Some clothing was such a mix of scraps that people resembled walking quilts.

Industrialization and Beyond

After the Civil War ended in 1865, America became increasingly **industrialized**. The prices of manufactured products started to drop. As items became cheaper and easier to get, people bought more of them. And they left farming to work in cities in industry, to earn more money. Now that people were working away from home, they looked for ways to save time. They would buy bread rather than bake it. They could afford new shirts instead of patching old ones. Families bought a lot more packaged goods.

industrialized: when there is a lot of manufacturing. Products are made by machines in large factories.

suburb: where people live near a city.

ration: limiting the amount of something to be used each week or month.

Using all of these new products created more and more garbage.

After World War II ended in 1945, Americans experienced new wealth. Many moved out of the cities to large, growing **suburbs**. Advertisers created ads and commercials that urged people to buy more of their new and improved products. Disposable items promised people cheap convenience. Americans bought into the hype. And so it continues right through to today.

Where are we going to dump all of this when we're done with it? How will all this garbage affect our environment—and our future?

During World War II, Americans on the home front pitched in to help the war effort. They **rationed** food and gas and planted victory gardens to grow fruits and vegetables. From coast to coast people chanted, "Use it up, wear it out, make it do, or do without."

Investigate a Mini Midden

Pretend you're an archaeologist from the future. Dig into a wastebasket from the present and carefully examine the artifacts you find. What do they tell you about how people live today? Make sure to be careful of sharp items in the trash.

1. Before you begin, come up with a list of questions to guide you in your investigation. Jot them down in your notebook. You might include questions such as: Who used these items? What animals did they live with? What foods did they eat? How did they dress?
2. In your journal, make a chart with three column headings: Sketch, Description, Use.
3. Spread the tarp and carefully unload the wastebasket onto it. Beware of anything sharp or broken as you carefully separate the items.
4. For each item, complete the chart. Write a description and make a quick sketch. Then think about how the item might have been used and who used it.

SUPPLIES

- notebook and pencil
- tarp or plastic sheet
- full wastebasket

Trash Flash

Over 2,000 years ago, the people of Pompeii in Italy tossed reeking rubbish and human waste into the streets. Workers paved the streets and walkways with rugged steppingstones. As people strode from stone to stone, they stayed high and dry. Their robes and sandals didn't slosh through the goo.

5 Once you're finished with your excavation, look again at the list of questions you wrote down and draw conclusions about the folks who produced this rubbish.

Hint: Ask permission from a family member to investigate his or her wastebasket. That way, you'll explore unfamiliar stuff discarded by others.

JUST For Fun!

How did Farmer Brown mend his tattered overalls?

With a cabbage patch.

ACTIVITY

Dig It!

Bury Artifacts in a Shoebox Model

Archaeologists dig through layers of soil to scout for artifacts. Bury artifacts in a shoebox, create layers, and peel away the box to reveal your own dig site.

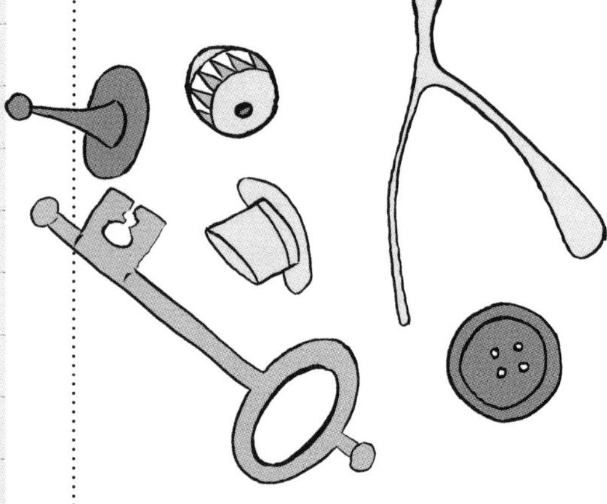

SUPPLIES

- small artifacts from your life such as: coins, keys, game pieces, jewelry, broken toys, washed chicken bones
- cardboard shoebox
- ½ cup cornstarch
- spray bottle with water
- large bowl
- dirt from outside (not potting soil)
- birdseed, sesame seeds, or sunflower seeds
- sand
- gravel or pebbles
- water
- plant parts: twigs, bark, leaves, grass, pinecones, pine needles, acorns, flowers
- scissors

1. Make the artifact layer. Spread your odds and ends along the bottom of the shoebox. Pour cornstarch into the bottle of water. Shake well. Spray the artifact layer with the water mixture.

2. In the bowl, combine most of the dirt with the seeds and spread it over the artifacts. Leave some extra dirt aside. Spray this soil layer with the water/cornstarch mixture until it has the consistency of a soggy mudpie. It should move and flow a bit.

3. Combine most of the sand and gravel or pebbles with water until it is moist. Leave some extra sand aside. Spread the mixture over the soil layer. Press down firmly so the materials stick together.

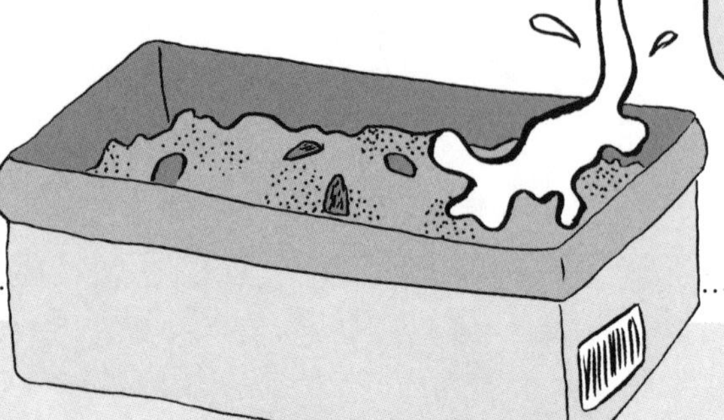

4 Combine the remaining dirt and sand. Spray with the water mixture and press onto the sand layer. Then sprinkle plant parts over the top. Set the shoebox aside and wait three full days for your model to dry thoroughly. If you live in a dry area, it might not take three days. If you live somewhere humid, it could take longer.

5 When the model has dried, use the scissors to cut down the corners of the shoebox. Leave the bottom of the shoebox intact. Carefully pull away all four sides of the box to unveil your model.

Hint: If your layers aren't sticking together well enough, add a bit more cornstarch to the water to thicken it.

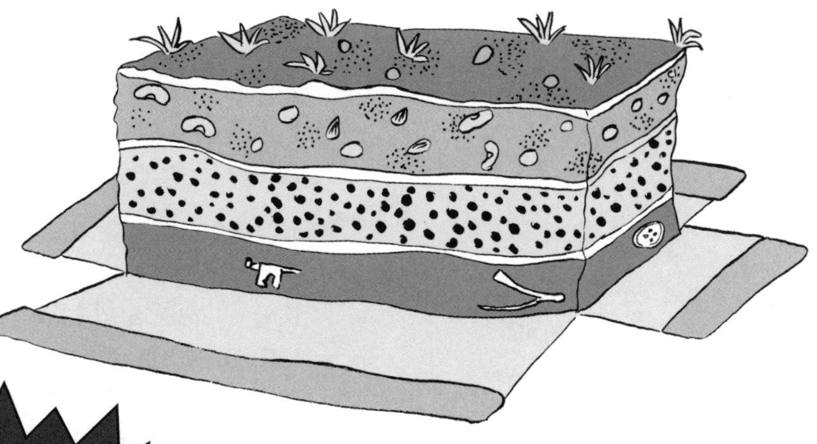

Trash Flash

The ancient Maya reused and recycled. They salvaged hunks of broken pottery from homes and stones from buildings. They gave these bits and pieces new life by reusing them to construct temples. The Maya also reduced their use of resources in burial practices. Instead of burying the dead with solid gold earrings, bracelets, and necklaces, they wrapped gold foil around clay beads to make fabulous fakes that looked like the real thing.

To Dye For!

Has your old T-shirt seen better days? No need to let it die. Dye it instead!

Next time your family boils colorful veggies, don't dump the water. Use it to brew natural dyes the way the colonists and pioneers did. Then use the dyes to jazz up your shirt and give it new life. Note that this activity requires using a stove to boil water, so have an adult help you.

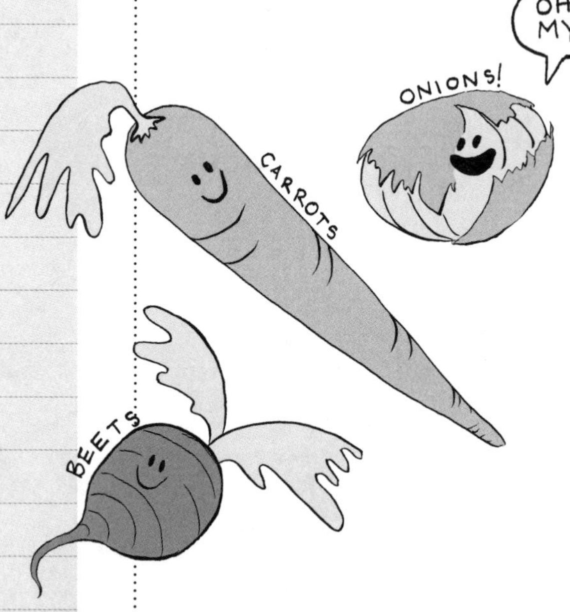

1 Choose your color. Wild about red? Beets do the trick. Carrots produce orange, naturally. Gold onions make yellow, red cabbage produces purple, and spinach gives you green. Put the vegetables in a pot and cover with water. Boil them, and then drain the colorful liquid and strain out any lingering solid bits. Store the liquid in a glass jar until you're ready to dye the shirt.

2 Before you use the colored liquid you'll need to make sure the dye will set and take hold in the fabric.To make the dye-set liquid, pour 4 cups of cold water (950 milliliters) and 1 cup of vinegar (240 milliliters) into the large pot. Place the T-shirt into the mixture. Then put the pot on the stove, and set the burner to simmer. Allow the shirt to simmer for a full hour, checking on it now and then to make sure the liquid doesn't boil away completely.

SUPPLIES

- colorful veggies like beets, carrots, gold onions, red cabbage, or spinach
- large pot
- stove
- water
- strainer
- glass jar
- cold water
- white vinegar
- cotton T-shirt
- rubber gloves

In the Middle Ages, dyers soaked fabrics in vats of old urine to set dyes!

Hint: When it's time to launder your completed veggie-dyed shirt, wash it separately in cold water. The dye will last longer and won't stain anything else.

3 After an hour, remove the shirt from the pot. Rinse it in cold water.

4 Now you're ready to work with the colored liquid. Return the pot and T-shirt to the stove. Pour in the colored water, and set the burner to simmer again. Keep an eye on the pot. When you are happy with the color, turn off the heat. Wear rubber gloves to handle the shirt because the dye will stain your skin. Keep in mind that the color will dry a few shades lighter than it looked in the pot.

Stench B-Gone Pomander

In colonial times, people used pomanders to ward off bad odors. Some people believed pomanders protected them from disease. Make a pomander with citrus fruit and cloves. It's a fantastic spicy air-freshener made with all-natural products. Have an adult help you make the holes in the fruit.

SUPPLIES

- thin nail or metal skewer
- medium-sized orange or large lemon
- ½ cup whole cloves (120 milliliters)
- 1 tablespoon cinnamon
- 1 tablespoon nutmeg
- 1 tablespoon allspice
- 1 tablespoon ginger
- brown bag
- 1 tablespoon orris root powder
- ribbon

1 Use the nail or skewer to pierce a pattern into the fruit. Try squiggles, zigzags, diamonds, or hearts. If you prefer, just pierce holes all over the entire orange.

2 Fill each hole with a clove. Each time you press a spicy clove into the fruit, you'll catch a whiff of mingled scents. Watch your fingers and pushing thumb. Cloves can be sharp and prickly.

3 When you're finished with the cloves, set the fruit aside. Pour cinnamon, nutmeg, allspice, and ginger in the brown bag. Add orris root powder, which preserves the pomander's scent. Shake the bag to mingle all the ingredients.

4 Place the fruit in the bag and roll it in the spices. Remove the fruit and tie the ribbon around it. Hang the pomander and allow it to dry out for about a week. Then hang it in the kitchen or a closet to freshen the air.

CHAPTER 3

Where Does Trash Go?

Take out the trash. Throw away the garbage. Dump the junk. Sooner or later, no matter where you live, you have to get rid of your rubbish.

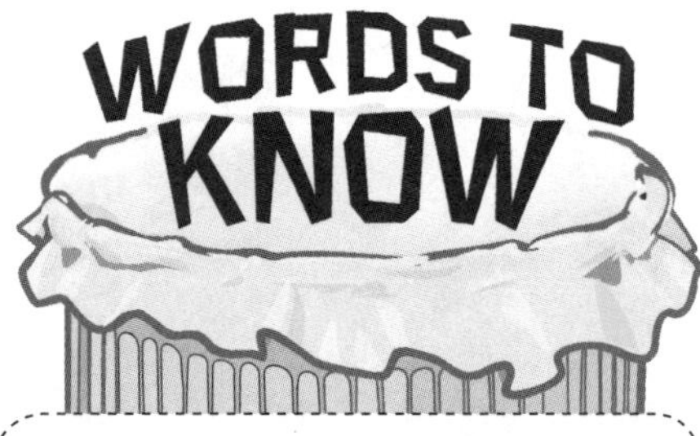

waste stream: the flow of household and industrial garbage that gets hauled away, recycled, incinerated, or disposed of in landfills.

sanitation worker: a person hired to collect and dispose of garbage.

compactor: a machine that tightly packs trash.

compress: to squeeze and squish things to make them smaller.

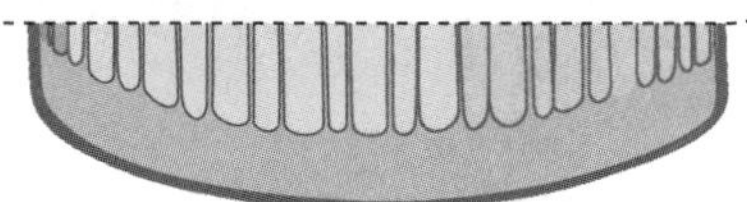

To Toss or Not To Toss?

An author named Susan Strasser wrote a book called: In *Waste and Want: A Social History of Trash*. She wrote, "Everything that comes into the home—every toaster, pair of trousers, and ounce of soda pop, and every box and bag and bottle they arrive in—eventually requires a decision. Keep it or toss it."

Once you make the decision to ditch something, it enters the **waste stream**. This is the flow of garbage to its final destination. Garbage can be recycled or burned. But the most common choice people make today is to dump it. So where does dumped junk actually go?

There's no magical spot where garbage vanishes in a poof. Away is somewhere. That somewhere is usually a landfill in people's towns and neighborhoods. You can see them from highways.

Trash Flash

How long does it take a **sanitation worker** to unload a mammoth garbage trailer? Only five minutes! In some places, garbage trucks transfer trash to barges, which are large boats with flat bottoms. Then tugboats push the barges across water to landfills.

Out and Away to the Landfill

If it weren't for landfills, you'd be slogging through slime. Your friends and family would be climbing over squishy, awful mounds of goo. As part of solid-waste management, garbage trucks pick up trash and haul it away to landfills. Imagine you're a sanitation worker in a rumbling truck named Bertha.

> **JUST For Fun!**
>
> What do you get when you cross a horsefly and a garbage truck?
>
> A stinkbug.

Bertha bellows a warning and chugs down long streets to visit every house and apartment building. You stop at each, picking up hefty cans and plastic bags and hurling them into the **compactor** at the rear of the truck. Like monster jaws, the compactor chomps and **compresses** the trash.

Trash Flash

Archaeologist William Rathje and his team of garbologists have excavated landfills since 1987. While digging through household rubbish, Rathje's team unearthed a 10-year-old head of lettuce. Why didn't the veggie decay? Because there was no air and water, which are necessary for biodegradation to occur. Which food took the longest to break down in crammed landfills with very little air? Hot dogs! Garbologists dug up hundreds of frankfurters, some of which were 27 years old. The team determined how old the foods were by studying newspapers crammed around foods in the landfill.

Bertha holds a gigantic 14 tons of waste (12½ metric tons). That's about as much trash as 850 households produce! When the truck is filled to the brim with compacted junk, you hit the landfill. Shrieking seagulls circle overhead. You blast your horn to shoo them away. Seagulls rummage through debris and send litter into the wind. Surrounded by the smell of rotting food, you dump your truckload into a **cell**. This is a storage space for garbage. Soon it's time to rumble off to another neighborhood and another stretch of waiting cans and bags of trash.

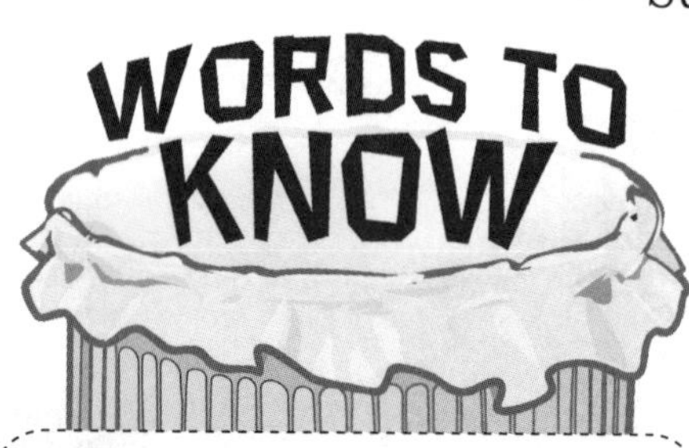

biodegradation: the process of materials naturally breaking down.

cell: a storage space for garbage in a landfill.

technology: tools, methods, and systems used to solve a problem or do work.

Parts of a Landfill

A landfill is more than just a dump. It's a garbage graveyard. On the surface, it looks like a gargantuan trash hill. As you've already learned, an open dump allows disease to spread, while a landfill protects the environment.

Engineers and scientists use current technology to design landfills that protect people and the environment.

It takes massive earthmovers to build a landfill. First, backhoes dig an enormous trench, or underground cell, about 200 feet wide and up to a half-mile deep (61 meters wide and 805 meters deep). This massive hole in the ground is the storage compartment for trash. The backhoes shove aside the removed soil to reuse later.

Trash Flash

New York's Fresh Kills landfill once towered at a height of 225 feet tall (69 meters). That's taller than the Statue of Liberty! After Fresh Kills closed in 2001, New York City needed to ship its trash away. Now, the city's garbage travels to landfills and incinerators in New Jersey, Virginia, Ohio, and South Carolina.

pesticides: chemicals used to kill pests like rodents or insects.

contaminant: a poisonous or polluting substance.

leachate: liquid produced in landfills as garbage decays.

groundwater: underground water supplies.

methane: a greenhouse gas produced by rotting garbage.

flammable: easily set on fire.

greenhouse gas: a gas such as water vapor, carbon dioxide, and methane that traps heat and contributes to warming temperatures.

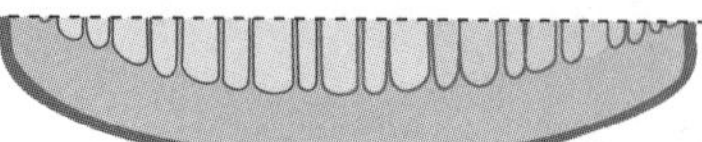

You can't just dump garbage into this hole, though. Trash often contains toxic materials like battery acids and **pesticides**. Other items, such as disposable tableware, leak **contaminants** as they break down. As waste decomposes, it produces **leachate**. This is a liquid that mixes with rainwater to brew a toxic soup.

To keep this toxic soup from seeping into the ground, the bottom of the landfill contains a layer of clay. This protects the soil and **groundwater** from contamination. On top of the clay layer is a heavy plastic liner for extra protection. Installed above the plastic liner is a layer of pipes. The pipes collect runoff rainwater and leachate.

The pipes serve another purpose. When garbage rots in the landfill, it releases a gas called **methane**. Methane is **flammable** and explosive if too much builds up in a contained space.

To reduce the danger of an explosion, pipes carry the methane outside where it is released into the air.

Landfills emit the **greenhouse gases** methane and carbon dioxide. Methane can provide energy. Some communities capture the methane coming from landfills and use it to generate heat and electricity.

After garbage trucks tip their loads into refuse cells, the landfill compactor attacks. At 84,000 pounds (38,102 kilograms) and armed with spiky metal wheels, this bad boy means business. The compactor rolls over the garbage again and again, squashing it to make room for more loads.

What do you call a snoozing bull?

A bulldozer!

When the compactor finishes its work, the bulldozer roars into action. Remember the soil the backhoes set aside? Now the bulldozer pushes this dirt and spreads it over all the garbage.

Landfill Compactor

This top soil layer, called daily cover, keeps hungry scavengers such as rats, raccoons, and coyotes from scrounging for supper. It also puts a lid on foul odors. In the morning, workers rev up their engines and start the process all over again.

JUST For Fun!

What do you get when an elephant skydives?

A giant hole for a landfill.

It takes about 30 to 50 years for a landfill to reach its **capacity**. When it's maxed out, waste disposal companies close it. Even when it's buried, decaying garbage can harm air and water, so companies keep a close eye on the closed landfill. In fact, local, state, and federal laws require a minimum **monitoring** period of 30 years.

So we're still layering our trash like people did back in Troy, and we're running out of room.

In 1990, there were 6,300 landfills in the United States. Now, there are only about 2,300. Another will close today because it's full. That's why it's so important to reduce, reuse, and recycle, so we jam way less stuff into garbage graveyards.

WORDS TO KNOW

capacity: the maximum amount something can hold.

monitor: to watch, keep track of, or check.

TRY IT!

Eye spy a closed landfill! Can you spot one? Once closed, a landfill can become part of your community. It could now be a grassy recreational area, such as a golf course, baseball diamond, or park. Some closed landfills become nature preserves or trails for running, walking, and horseback riding.

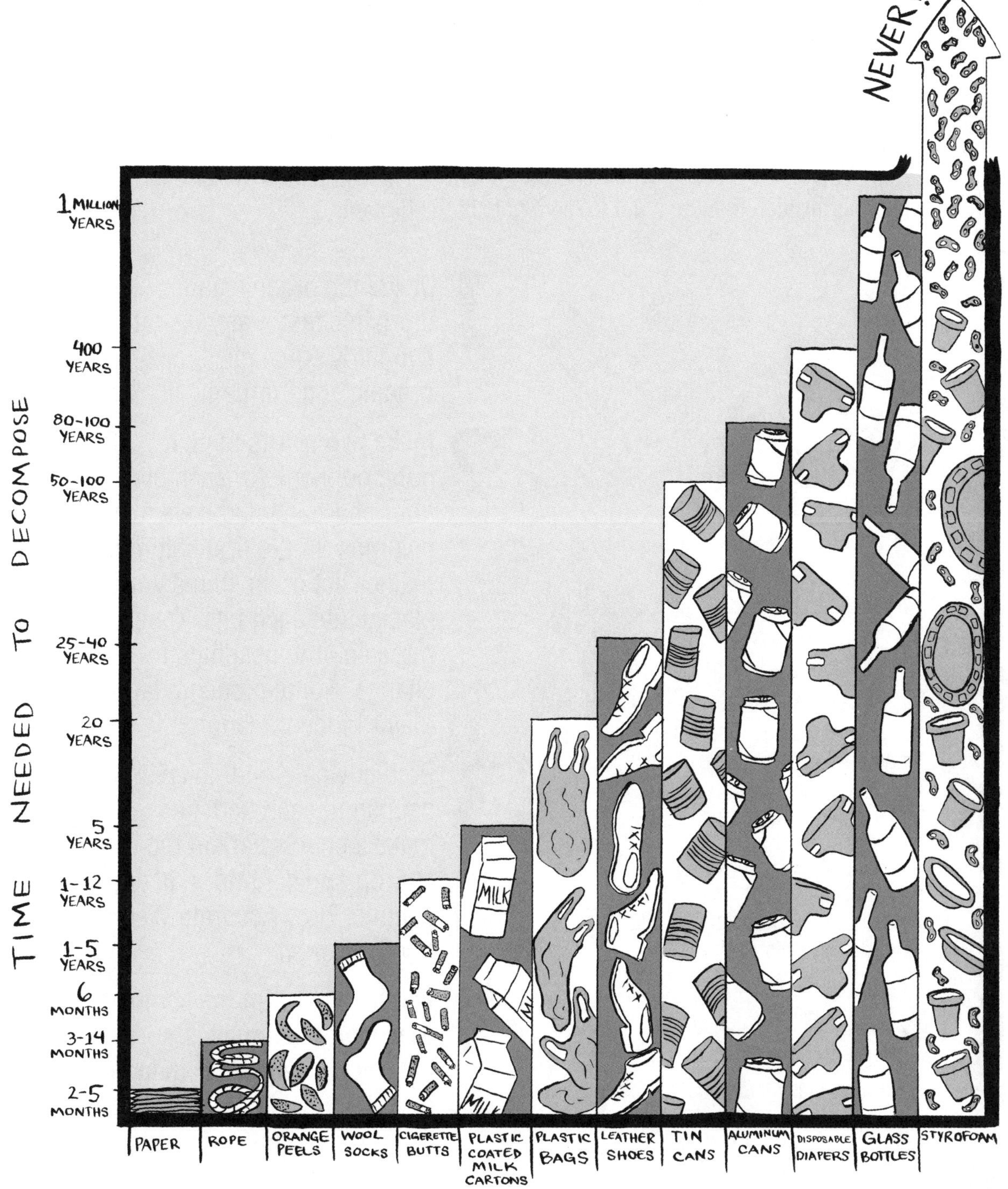
NEVER!
1 MILLION YEARS
400 YEARS
80-100 YEARS
50-100 YEARS
25-40 YEARS
20 YEARS
5 YEARS
1-12 YEARS
1-5 YEARS
6 MONTHS
3-14 MONTHS
2-5 MONTHS
TIME NEEDED TO DECOMPOSE
MILK
PAPER
ROPE
ORANGE PEELS
WOOL SOCKS
CIGERETTE BUTTS
PLASTIC COATED MILK CARTONS
PLASTIC BAGS
LEATHER SHOES
TIN CANS
ALUMINUM CANS
DISPOSABLE DIAPERS
GLASS BOTTLES
STYROFOAM
MATERIAL
SOURCE: AMERICAN FOREST & PAPER ASSOCIATION

Break It Down
With Biodegradation

Biodegradable materials decay and decompose with the help of bacteria and sunlight. Collect kitchen scraps for this two-week activity. Predict which items will break down most quickly when you bury them in test containers. Make sure you have permission from an adult to dig a hole in the ground.

SUPPLIES

- organic food scraps—apple cores, banana peels, cantaloupe and watermelon rinds, carrot and potato peels, coffee grounds, egg shells, etc.
- inorganic waste—aluminum foil, juice bag, metal bottle caps, plastic grocery bags, plastic wrap, small glass jar, Styrofoam, etc.
- pencil and notebook
- 2 paper grocery bags or 2 mesh produce bags (the kind that hold oranges or potatoes)
- permanent marker
- plastic tag like the ones found on bags of bread, buns, etc.
- place outside where you can dig a hole
- spade or shovel
- watering can
- tarp or plastic sheet

1. Divide the organic and inorganic test materials into two fairly equal piles, mixing organic and inorganic items.
2. Make two charts in your notebook, one for each pile. Your charts should have five columns. In the first column, make a list of the items you placed into each pile. Then add three column headings for: No change, Some biodegradation, Major biodegradation.
3. Predict what you think will happen to each item and make a check mark in the appropriate column. Add a last column, How Accurate Was My Prediction?
4. Fill the bags with the samples. Make sure materials are loosely packed rather than tightly squished together. Number the tags 1 and 2, and attach each to the appropriate bag.

5 Choose a spot outdoors to bury the bags. Dig two individual holes. Place each bag in a hole, and cover it completely with soil. Water each thoroughly. Every day for the next two weeks, sprinkle the ground where the bags are buried with 2 quarts of water (almost 2 liters).

Hint: Don't bury meat, fish, or bones, because hungry critters will dig up your experiment!

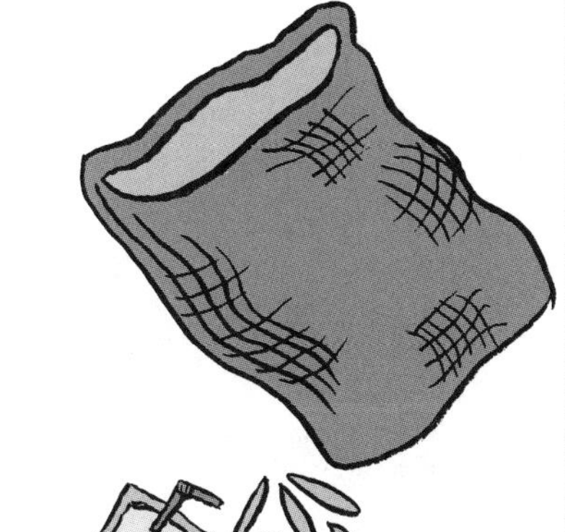

6 After two weeks, dig up the bags. Spread the tarp outside. Carefully shake out the contents of each bag. What do you observe? Worms or other creepy crawlies? Mushrooms and other fungi? Sulphury smells? Which items have shown signs of biodegradation?

7 Update your chart to fill in "How Accurate Was My Prediction?"

TRY IT!

Before you stash stuff in the bags, snap a picture. After two weeks, when you empty the bags, snap another. How do the pictures compare?

Snag Air Pollution on a Stick-It Can

What's hovering in the air where you live? Find out! Go outside and grab air pollution with a sticky can. What can you snatch in a week?

SUPPLIES

- 2 cans, such as Pringles containers or large soup cans
- permanent marker
- gravel and stones
- clear, double-sided tape
- magnifying glass

1. Select two equal-sized cans to reuse. Wash them and soak or peel off the labels before thoroughly drying.
2. Choose two different outdoor areas to test. How about the top of a tree stump in your yard or the ledge of a window near your apartment? Write the locations on the cans.
3. Fill the cans with gravel and stones to provide weight in them so they don't blow away outside. Then use double-sided tape to cover the outside of the cans. Try to keep your fingerprints, fuzzballs, and pet hairs off the tape. It's tricky!
4. Now you're ready to capture air pollution on your Stick-It Cans. At each outdoor location, use your senses to observe air conditions. What do you smell? How does the air look and feel? Are there factories or chimneys nearby? Burning leaves? Is someone grilling burgers?

What's the richest kind of air?

Gazillionaire!

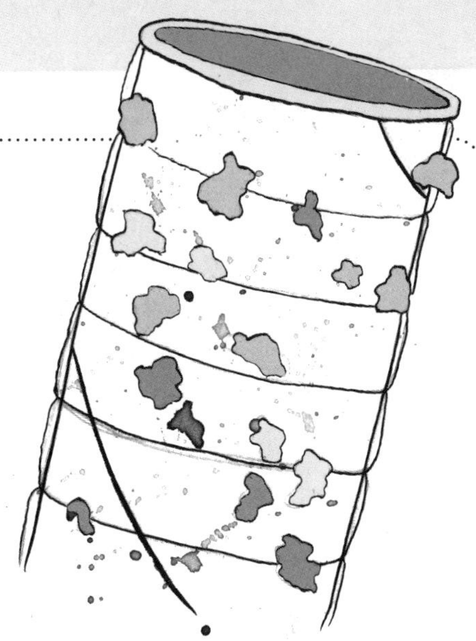

5 Wait a full week. You might want to check every day to make sure the cans haven't been disturbed. After a week, use the magnifying glass to study samples. What's stuck on the tape? Do you observe particles of ash, dust, or soot? How about bits of plants, pollen, or other items that aren't examples of pollution? Any liquids? Anything you can't identify? What could it be?

6 Compare and contrast the cans. Which sample grabbed more pollution? What outdoor conditions affected the results? Draw conclusions about your findings.

Trash Flash

When garbage gets incinerated, it doesn't just go up in smoke. Garbage can release chemicals like dioxin if it's not burned properly. That's the most toxic human-made substance on the planet. In addition, ash is left behind and needs to be disposed of—in a landfill.

dioxin: an extremely toxic chemical that can be released from burning some materials.

Simulate Water Pollution

Landfills are designed to seal in wastes that might contaminate water. Yet toxic dust can still escape and blow into water sources. These pollutants can quickly spread, sinking into soil and washing up on beaches. In this experiment, use a stalk of celery to find out how plants take in and circulate water pollution. Have an adult help you cut the celery.

SUPPLIES

- clear glass jar
- water
- red or blue food coloring
- 1 teaspoon dirt
- spoon
- stalk of light-colored celery with leaves
- cutting board
- knife

1 Fill the jar halfway with water. Add eight drops of food coloring. Red or blue will work better than other colors for this activity. Imagine that the color is a pesticide that flowed from a backyard into a pond.

2 Carefully pour dirt into the jar and stir the mixture. Think of the dirt as cigarette ashes that picnickers ditched in the pond.

3 Choose a stalk of celery that's light in color and has its leaves. Wash the stalk to remove any traces of dirt. Then place it on the cutting board and cut off a bit of the bottom. Pretend the celery is a healthy tree growing at the water's edge. Place the stalk into the jar with the leaves pointing up. Allow the celery to remain in the water overnight. What do you predict will happen?

4 The next day, take the celery out of the jar and study it. What happened to the leaves? To the stalk? The leaves should have changed color. Place the celery on the cutting board and cut away several samples to study. Do you see colored lines or dots of dirt in the stalk's veins? What conclusions can you draw about water pollution?

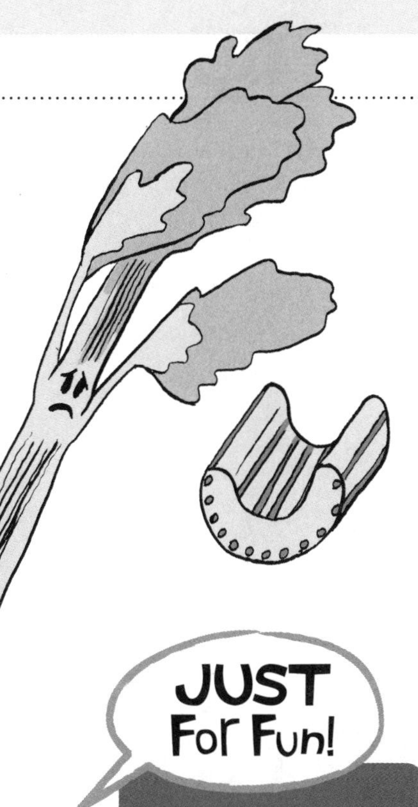

JUST For Fun!

What do you call a nervous celery stalk?

An edgy veggie!

Trash Flash

Nothing survives in a dead zone. Dead zones are areas in the world's oceans where oxygen levels are so low that life can't be sustained. Every summer, a dead zone the size of New Jersey forms in the Gulf of Mexico. Cow poop and chemical fertilizers from farms in the Midwest wash into the Mississippi River. They create the marine wasteland when they seep into groundwater and flow to the Gulf. There, chemicals cause massive algae growth. As blankets of algae decompose, they suck oxygen from the water. Fish and shrimp have to move to cleaner waters to breathe. Sadly, they don't all make it. During the summer of 2010, thousands of fish died in the Gulf of Mexico. The dead zone became a carpet of dead fish.

Whip Up an Edible Landfill

Landfills are layered with garbage and soil. In this project, you'll use yummy ingredients to make your own landfill model. When this salty-sweet landfill closes, you get to eat it! Note that this experiment uses an oven, so have an adult help you.

SUPPLIES

- oven
- pie pan
- ziplock freezer bag
- 20 graham crackers
- rolling pin
- measuring cup
- mixing bowl
- 2 tablespoons sugar
- 6 tablespoons butter
- small bowl
- microwave
- spatula
- 2 boxes instant butterscotch pudding
- milk
- 8 fruit strip pieces
- 2 gingersnaps, crushed
- 10 thin pretzel sticks
- ¼ cup raisins (30 grams)
- ¼ cup nuts (20 grams)
- chocolate sprinkles
- green sprinkles

1. Preheat the oven to 350 degrees Fahrenheit (177 degrees Celsius).

2. Imagine that the pie pan is a newly dug landfill. First, you're going to make a graham cracker crust that represents the protective clay layer. Place about 12 graham crackers into the ziplock bag and squash them with the rolling pin. Measure and crush more crackers until you have 1½ cups of crumbs (150 grams).

3. Pour the crumbs into the mixing bowl and add sugar. Melt the butter in a small bowl in the microwave and add to the crumbs. Use your hands or the spatula to blend the ingredients. Then, with the spatula and your fingertips, press the dough all around the pie pan. Bake the crust for 8–10 minutes, and allow it to cool completely.

4 In the meantime, follow the directions on the pudding box to combine the mix and milk. Set aside. Then line the cooled crust (the clay layer) with the fruit strips. These are the landfill's soft plastic layer.

5 Flatten ginger snaps inside the ziplock bag. Then scatter the crumbs over the fruit strips. This is the gravel that holds down the plastic layer. Then place pretzel sticks horizontally over the "gravel." These are pipes that collect ater and methane gas.

6 It's time to tip loads of garbage into your landfill. Fill the pan with a layer of pudding. This represents food scraps and yard waste. Then shake on raisins and nuts. These are reusable and recyclable bits and pieces.

JUST For Fun!

Which snakes slither over the front of garbage trucks?

Windshield vipers!

7 Add another layer of pudding for more scraps and waste. Now shake chocolate sprinkles on top to represent the daily soil cover. Finally, drizzle on the green sprinkles. This is the grass growing over your closed landfill.

ACTIVITY

CHAPTER 4

Hazardous Waste

Some of our trash is waste that harms people, animals, and the environment. Items that contain toxic and chemical materials sometimes make their way into our landfills. This harmful trash is called hazardous waste.

What does hazardous waste make you think of? Maybe it's toxic **runoff** that trickles out of parking lots and splashes into rivers. Or nasty **sewage** that floods beaches during heavy rains. Surfers in southern California got sick with ear infections, skin problems, and stomach bugs after unusually heavy rains in early 2011.

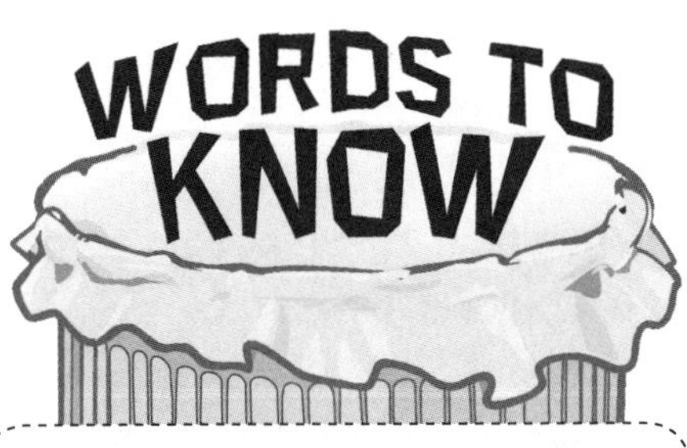

hazardous waste: chemical or toxic materials such as pesticides and paint thinners that hurt people, animals, and the environment.

runoff: produced when water picks up wastes as it flows over the surface of the ground. Runoff can pollute streams, lakes, rivers, and oceans.

sewage: waste from buildings, carried away through sewers. A sewer is a drain for waste.

catastrophic: involving or causing large amounts of damage.

sludge: oozy waste materials in sewage.

rupture: to burst or break suddenly.

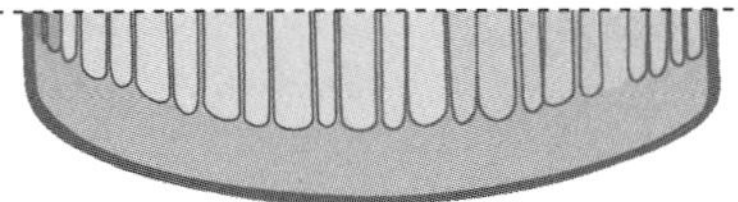

Perhaps hazardous waste makes you think of catastrophic events.

In October 2010, an environmental disaster occurred when toxic **sludge** flooded towns in Hungary, a country in eastern Europe. When the chemical waste reservoir at an aluminum plant **ruptured**, 35 million cubic feet of red sludge (1 million cubic meters) clobbered bridges and houses. It burned animals and people, and at least nine people lost their lives.

Under the Kitchen Sink

Hazardous waste is pretty dangerous stuff, right? And yet most of us are right at home with products that produce hazardous waste. We handle them all the time. They're stashed under kitchen sinks and tucked in bathroom cabinets. They're tottering on shelves in garages and garden sheds.

Trash Flash

In April 2010, a British Petroleum oil rig exploded and 11 people were tragically killed. The devastating spill spewed 184 million gallons of crude oil into the Gulf of Mexico (almost 700 million liters). Can you visualize this much water? According to the news group CNBC.com, it's enough to overflow 279 Olympic-sized swimming pools. That's how much oil spilled into the Gulf of Mexico.

The oil damaged ecosystems and coated marine birds and animals with oil. The spill also affected people who earn their living shrimping, fishing, and in other ways on the coast. One of the problems created by the spill was where to put all the oil after it was cleaned up. Whenever possible, BP shipped reusable oil to refineries. Unfortunately, much of the oily waste wasn't recyclable, so BP had to put it into landfills in several Gulf Coast states.

For example, drain cleaners that dissolve goopy hairballs contain chemicals that can be toxic. So does furniture polish and window cleaner. You'll find toxics in sweet-smelling hair spray, and stinky nail polish remover. Even your dog's flea powder contains chemicals.

Though we might not realize it, we frequently send the toxic chemicals from these household products out into the environment. We pour them into sink drains, flush them down toilets, and spray them off driveways.

Imagine a bustling Saturday morning on your street. In the driveway, one neighbor scrubs the tires of an antique Mustang with bubbly cleaner. Another neighbor sprays pesticides on prized roses, while a third refills the windshield fluid in his car, spilling some onto the curb.

When it rains, the toxic chemicals left behind from the bubbly cleaner, the pesticides, and the windshield fluid, mingle together. They flow into the gutter. Eventually the chemicals empty out into streams, lakes, and rivers, where they harm the environment.

Disposing of Hazardous Household Products

Household products that contain toxic chemicals require extremely careful handling. Paints, oils, and cleaners should be stored in a locked area away from people and pets, as the EPA recommends. This also helps to keep dangerous fumes out of your house.

You also have to be careful when throwing away hazardous products. Try to use up materials such as paints, or pass them along to someone who can finish them up. If they're dumped down drains they'll pollute water supplies. Tossed in the trash, hazardous waste will wind up in a landfill, where it will mix with leachate.

Find out when your community has a hazardous waste pick-up day. This is when toxic materials get hauled to special handling facilities.

Do you know people who change their own motor oil? Encourage them to recycle used oil at a service station or repair facility. According to the American Petroleum Institute, 2 gallons (7½ liters) of recycled motor oil can generate enough electricity to power your house for 24 hours. Discarded oil from a single oil change pollutes 1 million gallons of freshwater (4 million liters), enough to fill 20,000 bathtubs!

Medical Waste

Have you ever wondered where diseased lungs and gnarly warts wind up after doctors remove them? How about rotten teeth that dentists yank out? Or the needles that the vet uses for your cat's shots? It becomes **medical waste**. Health-care facilities, including hospitals, doctors' offices, and vets' clinics, all produce medical waste. By law medical waste must be placed in special containers marked "Biohazard." Hazardous-waste haulers remove the contents for safe disposal.

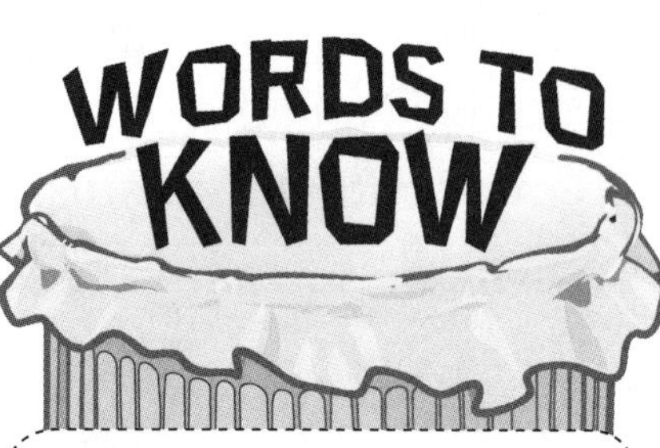

medical waste: waste generated at hospitals and doctor's offices, such as needles, bandages, or blood.

When not properly disposed of, medical waste can threaten public health. In 2009, syringes and biohazard bags washed up on a New Jersey beach during the Fourth of July weekend. Beach patrols quickly herded swimmers out of the ocean before clearing away the toxic debris.

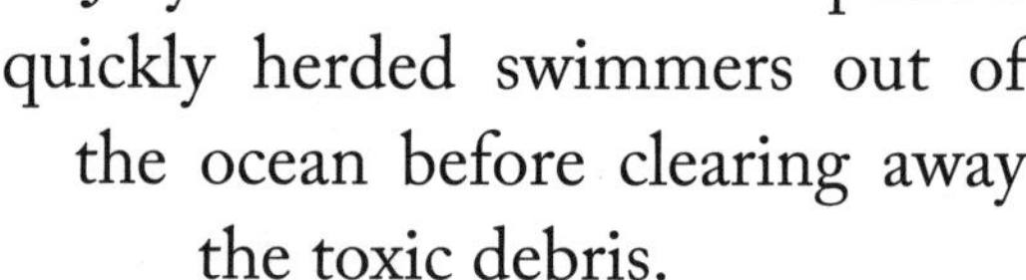

Rubbish Warriors

The Great Lakes are among our most precious natural resources. Sadly, much of the shoreline along these lakes is polluted. So a group of Midwestern kids and teachers decided to do something about it. They're part of the Alliance for the Great Lakes' Adopt-a-Beach program. The volunteers clean up littered beaches in Michigan, Minnesota, Ohio, and Wisconsin. In just one year, volunteers scooped up 186,000 soggy cigarette butts and cigar stubs!

The kids also remind picnickers, swimmers, and boaters not to litter.

After a group of students in New York City pitched in to help clean up local beaches, they wrote to the Ocean Conservancy in Washington, D.C., to share their observations. Jack, one of the kids, wrote, "I don't want to sound like I'm bossing people around, but you guys have to step up and get tough about this stuff."

Trash Flash

Used to fill cavities, amalgam is a silver-colored mixture of mercury, tin, silver, copper, zinc, and other metals. Mercury is toxic and can cause mercury poisoning. Although generally considered safe for cavities, amalgam can't just be thrown out when it's old. Dentists must recycle it.

Clean Up an Oil Spill

Cleaning up an oil spill is extremely challenging. Water currents spread the oil across waves and over beaches, which are nearly impossible to clean. When marine birds and mammals are "oiled," their feathers and fur lose the protective coating that makes them waterproof. As they groom themselves, they gulp down oil and die.

Sorbents are materials used to absorb liquids. Create an oil spill and test how different sorbents are able to clean it up. Then use feathers to simulate oiled birds.

SUPPLIES

- clear plastic tub
- water
- blue food coloring
- 1 teaspoon salt
- wooden spoon
- small mixing bowl
- ¾ cup vegetable oil (180 milliliters)
- 8 tablespoons cocoa powder
- sorbents to test: Brillo pads, paper towels, cotton balls, rags
- tweezers
- feathers
- 2-3 squirts of liquid dishwashing detergent

1 Fill the tub with clean water. Depending on the size of the tub, add 6–10 drops of food coloring. Mix in salt and stir.

2 In the mixing bowl, combine oil and cocoa powder to represent crude oil. You'll need to stir for quite a while to dissolve the oil and blend the ingredients.

3. Carefully pour the oil mixture into the tub of water. Pour gently and slowly, or the simulation won't work. Observe whether the oil floats or sinks when you add it to water.

4. Before you test the sorbents, predict which will be most successful in cleaning up the spill. Why do you think so? Then test each sorbent individually by carefully placing it in the center of the water. Observe what happens before you remove it with tweezers. Does the sorbent soak up the oil? The water? Does it float or sink? What conclusions can you draw?

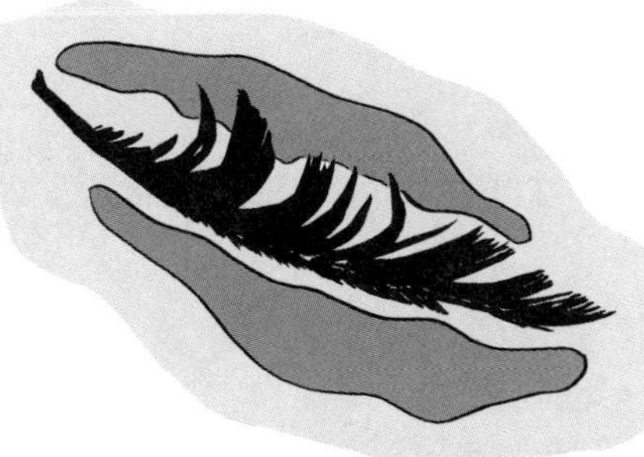

5. Add feathers to represent seabirds. Press the feathers into the water with the spoon and observe what happens. Do they float or sink?

6. Squirt in dishwashing liquid to spread the oil. Use the tweezers to remove the feathers. Wash the feathers with rags and paper towels. What happens?

Why did the pelican cross the beach?

To get to the other tide!

ACTIVITY

Compare Cleaners

What's lurking under your kitchen sink? Many common household cleaners are harmless, but others contain chemicals that could be hazardous. Can homemade, natural cleaning products work as effectively as commercial ones? You be the judge! Be careful and have an adult's permission to do this project. Use only the cleaners listed below.

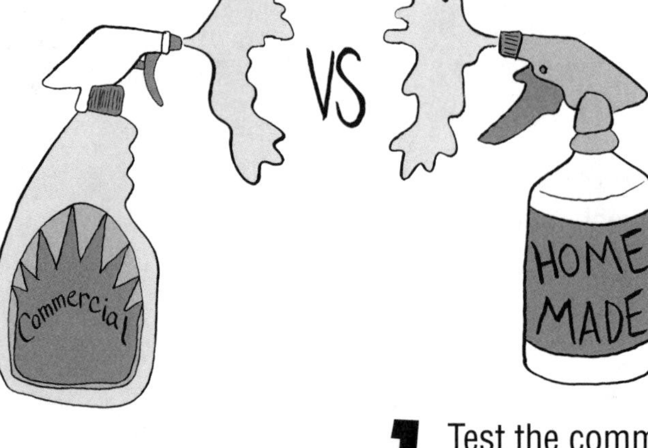

SUPPLIES

- commercial glass cleaner, like Windex
- rags
- newspapers
- 2 plastic spray bottles
- commercial wood furniture polish, like Pledge

Glass Cleaner Recipe

- 1 quart warm water (1 liter)
- ¼ cup inexpensive white or apple cider vinegar (60 milliliters)
- 2 tablespoons lemon juice

Wood Furniture Polish Recipe

- ¾ cup inexpensive olive oil (177 milliliters)
- ¼ teaspoon inexpensive white or apple cider vinegar

1. Test the commercial glass cleaner first. Spray it onto a window and use rags or newspaper to wipe the surface. How well does the product work? What are its strengths or weaknesses?

2. Combine warm water, vinegar, and lemon juice for your natural cleaner. Vinegar is a mild acid, and lemon juice is a citric acid that adds a clean, fresh scent. Pour the mixture into one spray bottle and test it on another glass surface. How does the homemade product compare with the commercial one?

Hint: These recipes contain items that spoil. Use up the homemade cleaners on other glass and wood surfaces within a few weeks.

3. Select a wood table or cabinet to test the commercial furniture polish on. What do you observe?

4. Combine the olive oil and vinegar in the other spray bottle. Test a tiny area of another surface to make sure the cleaner doesn't hurt the finish. Then, polish the surface. How does it compare with the commercial product? What conclusions can you draw about all the products?

JUST For Fun!

Knock-knock!

Who's there?

Distressing!

Distressing, who?

Distressing has way too much vinegar!

Experiment with Detergents

When we dump detergents into the environment, it can have an impact on the way plants grow. In this two-week project, test household products to discover how plants respond. Be careful handling detergents and get an adult's permission to do this project.

SUPPLIES

- permanent marker
- 3 of the same plants of equal size in plastic containers, such as beans, marigolds, and ivy
- ruler
- notebook
- ¼ cup (60 milliliters) each of 2 different commercial detergents, for example, liquid laundry detergent and powdered dishwasher detergent
- 3 jars with lids
- water

1. Label the plastic containers containing the plants. Write "Control" on one. Label the second with the name of one of the detergents and the third with the name of the other detergent. Label each jar in the same way. Measure the height of each plant, then jot it down in your notebook and add the date next to it.
2. Water the control plant with ¼ cup plain water from the jar marked control.
3. Work with the first detergent. In the appropriate jar, combine the detergents and ¼ cup water. Cover with the lid and gently shake the mixture. Pour it into the appropriately labeled plant.
4. Repeat step 3 with the second detergent. Then place all three plants in a sunny location.
5. For two weeks, sprinkle the Control plant with water every other day. Sprinkle the other two plants with more detergent-and-water mixture. After two weeks, assess the results.

JUST For Fun!

Why won't the giraffe wash with detergent?

She doesn't want to come out spotless!

6 Measure each plant, and compare the measurement with its starting height. How did each plant do? What conclusions can you draw about the impact of detergents on plant growth?

Trash Flash

In the early 2000s, runoff from dishwashers turned Washington State's Spokane River a gross shade of green! Why? Phosphates from dishwasher detergents promoted algae growth, which gave the river its green color. The algae then used up all the oxygen in the water, creating an aquatic wasteland like a dead zone. In 2006, clean-water activists rallied for a statewide ban on household phosphates. They succeeded and now the United States government has banned these phosphates for use in household products in all 50 states.

Reduce

The future of the earth's environmental health doesn't have to be all doom and gloom. We can focus on opportunities for change and new ways to use our valuable resources wisely.

The great news is that we're in charge of our choices and our actions. We choose what to buy, how to use it, and how to dispose of it. We share this planet, just like we share a snack of chips and salsa. And we can all pitch in to take care of our planet now, and for the future.

The first step is to reduce the amount of materials and products that we use.

Reducing what we use preserves Earth's resources and cuts down the amount of garbage we send to landfills. In the first chapter, you discovered how much waste your family produces. Now it's time to reduce it!

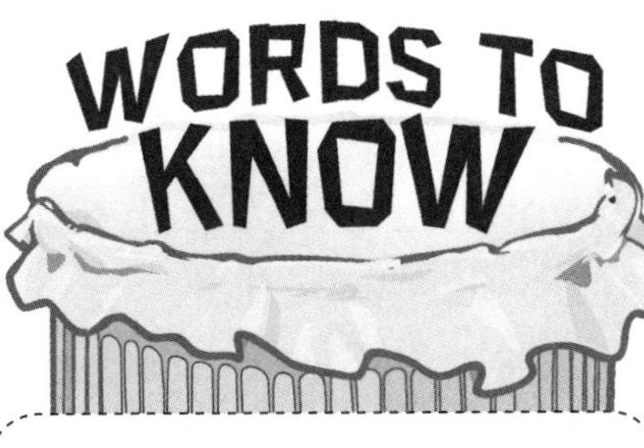

sustainability: living in a way that uses resources wisely, so they don't run out.

Sustainability

Lately, it seems like everyone's tossing around the word **sustainability**. But what does it mean? Sustainability is living in a way that uses Earth's resources very carefully. We don't want them to run out, so we can't use our resources up without concern for the future.

In 2008, the World Wildlife Fund (WWF) issued an alarming report. "If our demands on the planet continue to increase at the same rate, by the mid-2030s we would need the equivalent of two planets to maintain our lifestyles." Two planets! Clearly, our way of life isn't sustainable. It eats up Earth's resources without replacing them. Our lifestyle pollutes the air and water. We bulldoze land to build landfills and then jam-pack them with our waste.

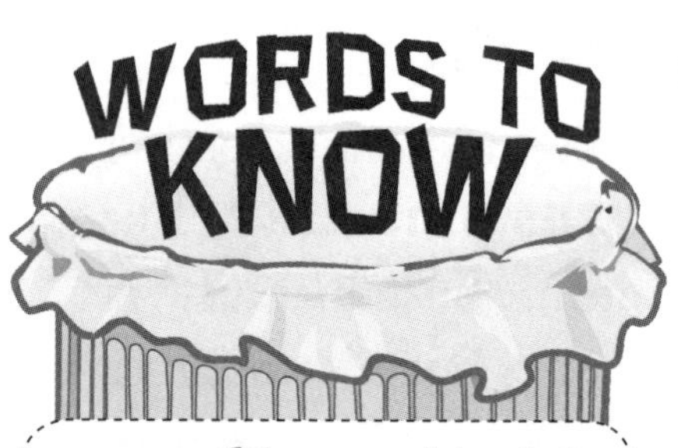

renewable: something that can be replaced after we use it.

exhaust: use up.

precycling: buying less and creating less waste.

processed food: food that has added ingredients to make it look nicer, taste better, last longer, or cost less.

Earth gives us everything we need to live: air, food, water, and warmth. Earth's gifts are a natural part of our lives. Sometimes we take them for granted and expect them to always be available—especially the **renewable** ones. Renewable resources, like water, timber, and fish, can be replaced after we use them.

But renewable doesn't mean never-ending.

What happens if we use up all the water in dry regions before it's replaced? Or chop down forests faster than they can grow back? Or eat so much fish that they don't have time to reproduce? Right now we're **exhausting** our resources and not planning for the future. Earth's resources are not unlimited.

Precycle It!

Are you **precycling**? The prefix pre- means "before." Precycling is reducing waste by "rethinking" our purchases and buying less. Recycling is a good thing, but it takes resources to transport materials, melt them down, and then make new items. Precycling means that less needs to get recycled in the first place.

The New York Times reported that Americans chow down on 31 percent more packaged foods than fresh food. These **processed foods**, which are canned, frozen, or dehydrated, are often loaded with salt and sugar.

TRY IT!

Hey, have you ever checked out the ingredients listed on processed, prepackaged foods? Anything you recognize as real food? Or are most of the ingredients very long words that you can't pronounce? Just saying.

What your family buys can have a tremendous impact on waste. For instance, you might buy a handy grab-and-go package of pizza for lunch. It comes in a cardboard box. Inside is a plastic tray and a plastic sheet.

Mini crusts and shredded cheese fill compartments, along with a sauce pouch. There's a plastic bottle of water with a lid and a wrapped cookie for dessert. Tally all that packaging, and you rack up eight pieces of rubbish! And that's just your lunch. If you stop buying products like this, you take an important step in reducing waste.

Do It Yourself

Rethink grab-and-go. Plan ahead to reduce your reliance on processed and packaged foods. Get your chef hat on and do it yourself! For instance, make your own pizza at home with your family. Store a few leftover slices in reusable containers for your personal brand of grab-and-go. You don't even have to make the crust. Just buy the dough, roll it out, and add the toppings you like. It's easy! And not only do you drastically reduce waste and conserve energy, but you also enjoy incredible satisfaction. You made it yourself—with fresh ingredients.

Packaging and Source Reduction

What was your favorite birthday present? Did it come in a box with lots of plastic inside and a set of instructions? Where was it made? When manufacturers ship products long distances, they have to use extra packaging to keep them from getting squashed. Transportation requires more **fossil fuels** that cannot be replaced. What did you do with the packaging? Throw it out? Keep it? Recycle it?

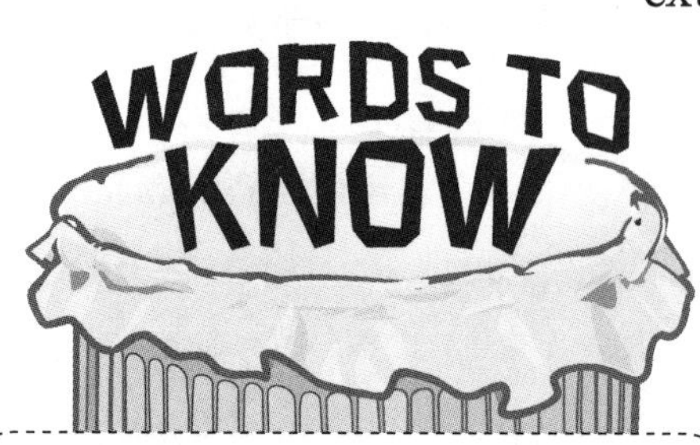

fossil fuels: oil, coal, or gas that formed in the earth from decayed plants or animals.

source reduction: reducing the quantity of waste, especially in packaging, so there is less to dispose of.

preventive: stopping something before it happens.

compostable: a material that can break down and rot in a compost heap.

Packaging is one of the largest contributors to our waste stream. That's why many manufacturers are working on source reduction.

Source reduction is reducing the amount of waste at the source, or beginning, of the waste stream. Reducing packing materials means there's less to dispose of later.

Source reduction is **preventive**. It stops something from happening. In this case, it stops the production of garbage that you have to get rid of later. When manufacturers make lighter plastic bottles or thinner straws that require less plastic, for example, they cut down the amount that becomes waste later. If you can, buy in bulk, because that uses less packaging and fewer materials that need to be recycled.

Most of all, don't buy into the hype. Glitzy packages are fun and designed to grab your attention. They practically screech, "Pick me!"

Yet, they usually cost more and don't add to the quality of what's inside. When you can, buy items "bare," with no packaging at all. If that's not possible, then try to buy products with certified **compostable** or recyclable packaging. Reuse packaging whenever you can. And who needs disposable packaging anyway when you can bottle homemade jams, bake your favorite muffins, and grow your own tomatoes for salsa?

Trash Flash

Have you ever eaten SunChips? These chips used to come in biodegradable bags that were made of plants. Consumers loved helping the environment while crunching on their favorite snack. But the eco-friendly bags came with an unexpected twist. Noise pollution! The stiff bags produced a deafening racket and even inspired a Facebook page, "Sorry But I Can't Hear You Over This SunChips Bag." In 2010, the Frito-Lay company decided to ditch the bags and go back to the drawing board. They added a rubber-based sticky substance to hold the layers together. The new bags are quieter and still biodegradable. At least Frito-Lay could hear the complaints!

In the Garden, Not in the Garbage

When you toss organic waste into garbage cans, it ends up in a landfill. Squished in a cell, organic waste produces methane, a greenhouse gas. Why not try composting? Composting speeds up the breakdown of organic waste. It naturally decays with decomposers and gives something back to the planet: a pesticide-free fertilizer. So close the loop. Practice another R—rot!

WORDS TO KNOW

vermicomposting: using worms in composting to break down and recycle food wastes.

Build a contained compost heap in a garbage can. Your compost should contain three basic ingredients: greens, browns, and water.

Green items, like grass, contain nitrogen. Brown items, like dead leaves, are carbon-rich. They'll attract decomposers that hop to it and break down wastes. When you add water to organic materials, it helps them decay. And don't forget to toss in those SunChips bags!

What if you don't have a yard or room for an outdoor compost? You can still reduce the amount of stuff you chuck in the trash. Bring it indoors with **vermicomposting**. Worms are stellar recyclers. They munch more than their own weight in garbage each day, digest it, and release waste called casings. Casings mingle with decaying organic materials and produce a rich fertilizer.

Did you know that worms are toothless? Like birds, they use gizzards, which are muscular organs in the digestive tract, to crush and grind food.

Simple Ways You Can Reduce and Precycle

- put leftovers from dinner in reusable containers for lunch the next day
- send electronic birthday party invitations instead of paper ones
- use nonbreakable, reusable plates, cups, and silverware instead of paper or plastic for a picnic or when you have a group of friends over
- always have a reusable water bottle with you so you don't ever have to buy bottled water
- ask your parents to buy nuts and nut butters, grains, cereals, spices, oils, and pasta in bulk, and then store them in empty glass jars
- keep a reusable cup in the bathroom for rinsing after brushing instead of disposable paper cups
- don't use straws, just drink out of the cup
- compost your food waste
- use a dishtowel instead of a paper towel to clean up spills
- buy loose fruits and veggies instead of packaged ones
- buy only in recyclable packaging when you need to buy packaged goods

Build a Garbage Can Compost Heap

Try composting your greens and browns to reduce waste. Do not add any meat, bones, or fish.

1 Scout around to find an ideal location for your heap. Make sure it's in a protected, shady place not too close to your house. If it's too close, critters that are attracted to the heap might get into your house. Arrange the bricks, pallet, or pieces of lumber as a foundation for the garbage can. Place the can on top.

2 Compost needs a balanced diet. Put on gloves and divide green and brown materials into piles of equal size. Break, chop, or shred larger chunks of materials. First, spread a 6-inch layer of browns in the can (15 centimeters). Then spread a 3-inch layer of greens on top of the browns (7½ centimeters). Add several handfuls of soil over the greens. Use your hands or a shovel to carefully mix the layers.

SUPPLIES

- bricks, wood pallet, or pieces of 2-by-4-inch wood (5 by 10 centimeters)
- large plastic garbage can with holes punched or drilled several inches up from the bottom
- gloves
- greens: fruit and veggie scraps, coffee filters and grounds, eggshells, grass clippings, teabags
- browns: autumn leaves, bark, branches, hay, straw, twigs
- soil
- garden hose
- rope or bungee cord

3 Add another 3-inch layer of greens (7½ centimeters) and some more soil. Wet but don't drown the heap. As a rule of thumb, keep the heap as wet as a damp sponge. Close the lid tightly, and use rope or bungee cord to secure it. That will keep hungry animals from scavenging.

Hint: It will take trial and error to discover the ideal mix of greens and browns. Equal parts might not work for you. If not, then vary the ratio. Try three parts browns to one part greens, and observe the results.

4 Get rolling! Your heap needs air and water to thrive. Once a week, place the garbage can on its side and roll it like a barrel to mix the layers. Check to make sure the heap is moist. As bacteria breaks down waste, they produce heat, so you'll notice that the compost warms up.

5 Once the heap is up and running, regularly add green and brown organic waste to keep the compost cooking. Add some soil each time and keep it moist.

6 Depending on where you live and what the surrounding conditions are like, it will take from 1 to 6 months for your compost to cook. When it's ready, the materials will look like rich, dark soil—black gold! You're ready to spread your all-natural fertilizer in flowerbeds or use it for outdoor potting soil.

Trash Flash

What keeps a lot of us from composting? The Ick Factor! When you throw food scraps into a garbage can, they're out of sight, out of mind. With composting, not so much. You get down and dirty. No doubt about it, food scraps are stinky and gooshy. How can you fight the Ick Factor? It takes time. And garden gloves work wonders. If you just can't get beyond the Ick Factor, find out if your community provides food scrap containers and curbside pick-up for composting.

Become a Worm Farmer

Red wigglers work the best in this worm farm!

SUPPLIES

- small, non-transparent plastic storage tub or organizer box with a lid—worms like things dark, so if you only have a see-through container, then cover the outside with black construction paper to block out light
- shredded black and white newspaper — colored or glossy pages can harm worms
- spray bottle of water
- soil
- red wriggler worms from a bait store or worm farm
- small food scraps: fruit and veggie leftovers, coffee grounds, crushed eggshells, teabags and tea leaves
- bits of houseplant clippings
- bricks or wooden blocks
- tray for drainage collection

Include on the Worm Menu

- small amounts of coffee grounds
- thoroughly crushed eggshells
- fruit and veggie peels and scraps
- teabags (remove metal staples or attachments) and tea leaves

Don't feed worms

- animal waste
- bones
- butter or oils
- egg yolks or whites
- fish or meat

1. Your worm farm needs good air circulation. Ask an adult to drill or punch several holes on the bottom (for drainage) and top of your container.

2. Make cozy, edible bedding for the worms. Use your hands to shred newspaper into 1-inch strips (2½ centimeters). Fill the container about halfway with fluffed-up newspaper. Spritz the bedding with water, but don't make it too soggy. Worms need moisture, but they'll die if conditions are too wet. Too much humidity might also invite pesky fruit flies.

3. You're ready to add 2 cups of soil (240 milliliters) to the bedding. Use your hands to thoroughly mix the soil into the newspaper. Then gently place the red wrigglers into the bedding. Worms love dark spaces, so give them time to burrow away from the light and into the bedding.

4 Once the worms have burrowed into a cozy spot, layer food scraps into the bedding. The smaller the scraps, the easier it is for worms to work their wonders, so chop or break up materials. Add another fluffy layer of newspaper on top to fend off yucky odors.

5 Worms thrive in temperatures between 55 and 75 degrees Fahrenheit (13 to 24 degrees Celsius). So put your farm in a shady, cool place away from direct sunlight. A basement, laundry room, or kitchen corner works well. A garage is great, too. Because there are holes on the bottom of the farm, it will drain. Place the farm on top of the bricks or wooden blocks with a tray underneath to collect drainage, called compost tea. The tea makes a nutritious treat for houseplants, so slip them a sip.

6 Check in with the worm farm every day. Make sure the bedding stays slightly moist. Add more food scraps. Over a period of about 3-6 months, worms will churn out rich compost. When it's time to remove the crumbly compost, coax the wrigglers to one side of the container. If you place some food in one area, the worms will wriggle to that spot. It might take a couple of days. Then carefully scoop out the compost from the other side. Add new bedding—and let the recycling continue.

7 It takes trial and error to keep the farm thriving. You might need to increase or decrease moisture or move the farm to a warmer or cooler location. Trust your powers of observation, and keep trying.

Hint: Don't use earthworms. They can't work on this farm, since they need a much deeper space to survive.

ACTIVITY

Grow an Avocado Plant

Holy guacamole! Don't pitch that avocado pit. Let it live on in a new plant. Ask an adult to help you with the toothpicks.

SUPPLIES

- avocado pit
- 4 toothpicks
- glass of water
- clay pot or planter, or pottery container to reuse
- potting soil

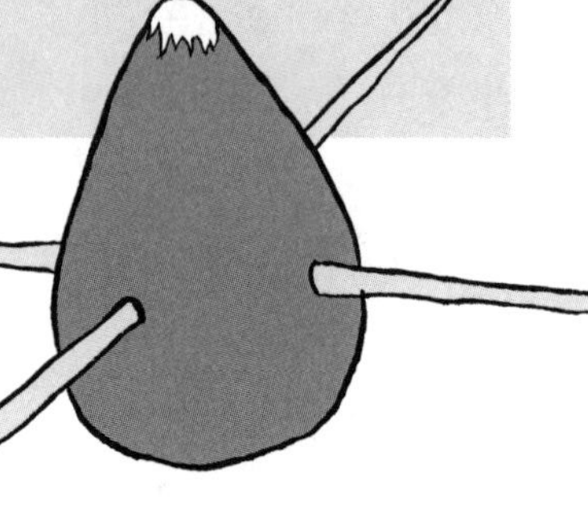

1. Under cool running water, wash the pit to remove any bits of avocado clinging to it. Gently blot it dry. Then, turn the pit so the wider end faces down and the pointy end is up. Carefully jab toothpicks into the pit, sticking one toothpick on each of the four sides.

2. Hang the avocado over the rim of the glass of water. Make sure there's enough water in the glass to submerge the pit about halfway.

3. Place the glass in a warm, sunny location, and check it every day. As the water level goes down, add more fresh water. After about a week, the brown layer of the pit will probably peel off and break away. In about two or three weeks, a root nub will pop from the bottom, and the pit will gradually split open. After about six weeks, a thin stem will spring from the upper part. In time, leaves will roll out from the stem.

4 When the leaves are about an inch long (2½ centimeters) you're ready to transplant. Fill your pot or planter with potting soil. Remove the toothpicks, and bury the roots and pit in the soil. Keep your plant in a sunny location, and water it regularly so the soil stays moist.

5 Avocado plants tend to get leggy. This means they grow spindly with leaves spaced widely apart along the stem. For a fuller plant, prune back the stem by snipping it with scissors when it gets to be about 4 inches high (10 centimeters).

TRY IT!

Grow a sweet potato vine using the same directions. Instead of a glass use a large jar filled with water, and use extra toothpicks if needed.

6 You can move your potted avocado plant outdoors in warm weather. Depending on what kind of climate you live in, you might be able to transplant it into the ground and grow a tree!

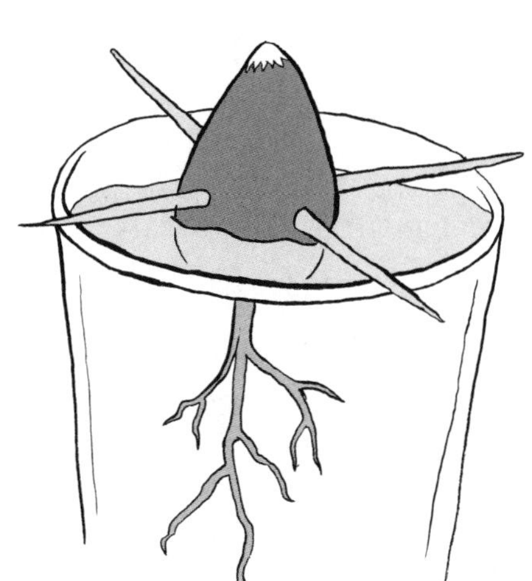

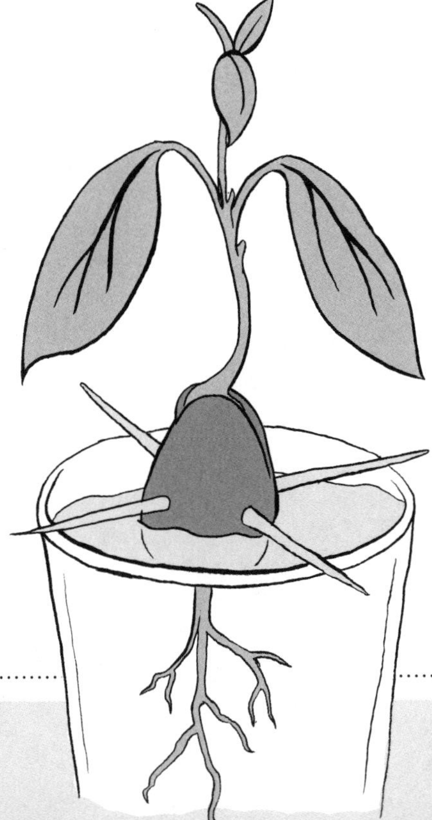

Reuse

So many products are at our disposal in a throwaway world. Diapers, tiny packets of mustard, paper napkins—they're designed to be used once for our convenience and then tossed out. We ditch the old to make way for the new. And we dump broken things instead of fixing them.

It can be easy to fall into throwaway thinking. But you don't have to be part of a throwaway world. Learn to reuse. This means saving things instead of throwing them out. Then finding new (and sometimes better!) ways to use them. You're not only keeping items from entering the waste stream, but you're using your creativity. Challenge yourself to consider stuff in a whole new way. What are some alternatives to throwing things out?

One option is to reuse items, even some disposable ones, in their original state. For example, if you use plastic plates, cups, and forks on a family outing, make them last. Wash and reuse them for the next picnic or camping trip. You can also wash ziplock bags repeatedly, and air-dry them on racks.

Trash Flash

Westward ho! When pioneers hit treacherous wagon trails to settle the West, they hauled as many possessions as they could manage. Along the way, pioneers found that they had to toss many of these things out to lighten their loads. Junk dealers followed their trails like ants after crumbs, looking for reusable treasure like clothes, furniture, and pots to sell.

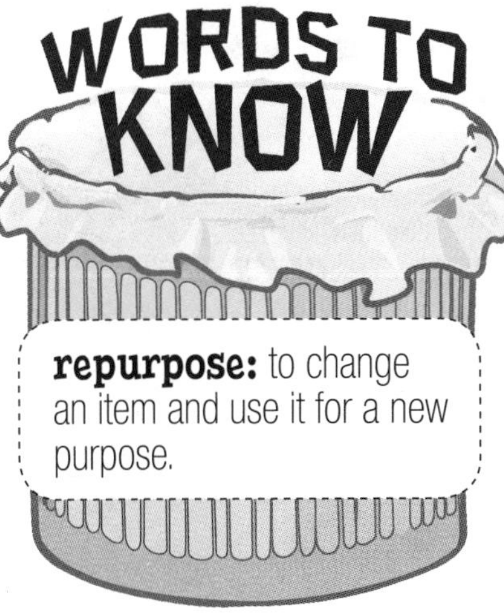

repurpose: to change an item and use it for a new purpose.

Instead of chucking broken items, fix them so they're better than ever. Repair rickety skateboards. Patch flat tires on your bike. Condition a dried-up baseball glove.

You can also **repurpose** stuff. This means taking old things and using them for something they weren't originally made for. For example, use empty glass jars from jams and nut butters to store dried beans, pasta, or oats. Cut the bottoms off different sizes of plastic bottles and use them as funnels. Or poke holes through an old garden hose to make a sprinkler. And instead of rolling an old tire into a landfill, use it for a tree swing.

Another way to reuse items is to donate them to charitable organizations such as Goodwill, the Salvation Army, and veterans groups in your community. Give magazines, books, and DVDs to nursing homes, shelters, and libraries. Find out if there's a Habitat for Humanity ReStore in your area. These resale shops accept gently used furniture, appliances, and building materials.

Easy Ideas for Repurposing

- paint empty coffee cans and use them for indoor planters
- line your veggie and fruit drawers with bubble wrap to prevent food from bruising
- dip an old bedsheet in water, wring it out so it isn't drippy, and hang it over your bedroom window when it's hot outside to cool down your room without using air conditioning
- use empty glass jars for storing all sorts of things including craft supplies, nails, screws, spare change, pens and pencils, and dry bulk foods
- use old sheets and quilts for picnic blankets
- scrub an old cutting board with half a lemon to refinish it
- screw vintage drawer pulls onto a chunk of wood to make a jewelry hanger
- mount dresser drawers on the walls to make bookshelves
- when it's time to replace a door, use the old one to make a desk or drawing table
- turn an old sink or even a bathtub into a big yard planter
- create a tote bag from a pillowcase
- convert old shutters to a bulletin board and tuck notes between the slats
- store holiday decorations and ornaments in empty egg cartons
- use wooden spoons and forks as plant stakes

Upcycle

Rummage through vintage, thrift, and consignment shops. Scout out garage and yard sales. Trade clothes with your friends. Then, give upcycling a whirl. Upcycling is different than recycling, which breaks down materials. And it's different than repurposing because when you **upcycle**, you take old materials and turn them into something not just different, but new and better.

WORDS TO KNOW

upcycle: to remake old products into something more environmentally friendly, and often of better quality and value.

For example, you can find old clothes in a thrift shop and make them fashionable. Add a fun border to the hem of an old pair of jeans. Turn old T-shirts into reusable shopping bags by sewing the bottom closed and cutting off the sleeves.

Sometimes it seems like an endless stream of stuff flows into our homes. Don't just throw it all out to a landfill when you're done with it. Remember, many items can be rescued and improved.

Trash Flash

Sticky notes, napkins, printer paper. How much paper do you use each year? According to the EPA, if you're like the average American, then it takes a 100-foot tall Douglas fir tree (30 meters) to make enough paper for you for one year! What changes can you make to reduce that amount?

Rubbish Warriors

It gleams like a crystal castle straight out of a fairy tale. But La Casa de Bottellas, a bottle house in Puerto Iguazu, Argentina, is a whole lot of garbage. Reused garbage, that is. The Santa Cruz family built this plastic palace with thousands of 2-liter plastic bottles. They used CD cases for windows. The ingeniously built bed, chairs, and shelves are also made of plastic. In all, they used 1,200 plastic bottles for the walls, 1,300 milk and wine cartons for the roof, 140 CD cases in the walls and windows, 120 plastic bottles for a couch, and 200 plastic bottles for a bed.

TRY IT!

What materials can you cobble together to build your own usable furniture—without buying anything?

Tips for Upcycling

- cut up an old vinyl or oilcloth tablecloth and make stylish lunch bags out of them
- use sweater sleeves to make fingerless gloves, and use the rest of the material to make a sweater for your dog
- snip wallpaper scraps and notebook paper to make miniature journals
- convert a leather belt into a wristband
- connect old watch faces to make a bracelet
- grow a terrarium inside an old lighting fixture
- clean out a yogurt container and cover it with fabric scraps and beads to make a gift box
- use colorful paint to jazz up an old accent table or chair
- use fabric paint on old canvas shoes to give them a new look
- glue old table legs to a suitcase to craft a storage table
- make covers for your textbooks with old T-shirts
- create mosaics with broken china and pottery or pieces of leftover tile
- craft a birdfeeder from a 2-liter plastic bottle and thin dowel rods for perches

Odds 'n' Ends Picture Frame

What's wasting away in your junk drawers? In this project, you'll decorate a picture frame with thingamajigs and doodads.

SUPPLIES

- wood or plastic picture frame to reuse
- odds and ends and found objects, including shells, acorns, broken toys and jewelry, foreign coins, and board game pieces
- optional decorations such as glitter, sequins, and beads
- Elmer's or other craft glue
- newspaper

Hint: Don't have a frame? Build your own out of old cardboard or glue together used Popsicle sticks.

1. Examine your objects. Do you notice a theme or pattern in your stuff? Or is it random? Decide how you want the items to be arranged on your frame and glue them on.
2. Place the frame on the newspaper to dry overnight. Make sure the side with the decorations is facing up. Check on the frame now and then. If any doodads have slipped out of place, nudge them back where they belong. Add more glue if needed.
3. When the frame has thoroughly dried, carefully peel away any glue drippings. Add a picture.

TRY IT!

Create frames to give as presents to your friends. What are they interested in? Sports? Animals? Theater? Try to find objects to glue on that reflect what your friends like to do.

Stash-It Locker Pocket

Reuse old jeans to make a stash-it pocket for your locker or fridge.

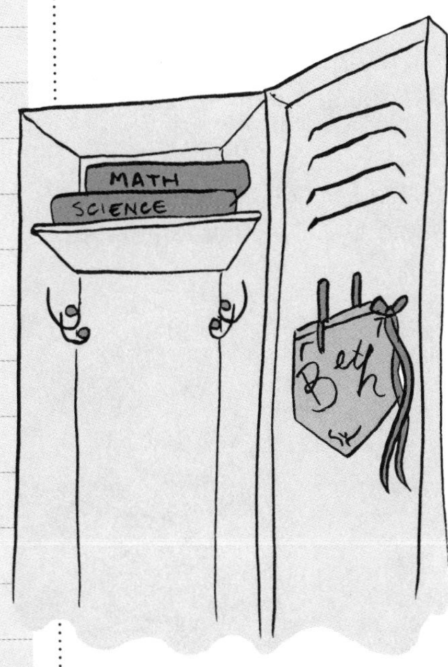

1 Work with jeans that have a pocket without any rips or tears. Snip away the pocket and the piece of pants that it's stitched onto. Try to cut as close to the fabric edge of the pocket as you can.

2 Spread out newspaper as a drop cloth. Use the fabric paint to decorate the pocket. Allow the paint to dry completely.

3 When the paint has dried, you can glue on whatever embellishments you want. Let the glue dry completely.

4 Flip over the pocket. If the magnetic strips have peel-away covers, remove them and position two strips on the sides of the pocket and the other two on the top and bottom. Otherwise, glue the strips in place.

5 Stick your Stash-It Pocket inside your school locker or on your fridge. Use it to hold pens, pencils, and other odds and ends.

SUPPLIES

- unwanted blue jeans
- scissors
- newspaper
- fabric paint
- Elmer's glue or fabric glue
- bits and pieces for embellishment—sequins, beads, charms, ribbons, etc.
- 4 magnetic strips

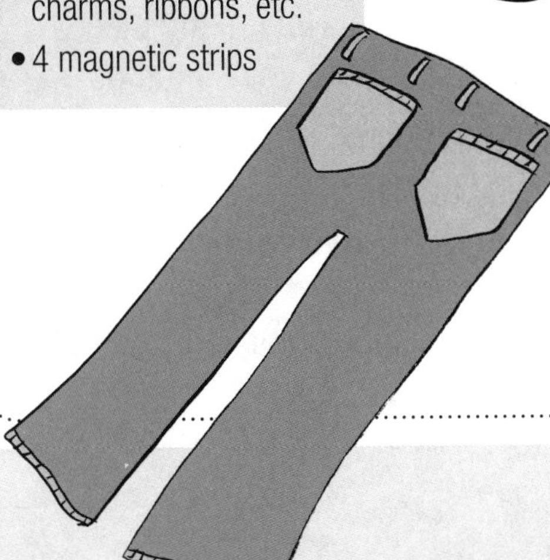

Beth

Junk Mail Bead Necklace

It's fun to get a card or package in the mail. But junk mail? Not so much. You don't ask for junk mail, but it shows up anyway. It's usually advertising materials like catalogs, flyers, credit card applications, and even CDs. One credit card company sends out materials in a fancy gold box with a plastic window, two Styrofoam bumpers, and five individual flyers inside!

Most families in the United States receive around 22 pieces of annoying junk mail a week. About 46 percent is never even opened. Many people toss it straight into the trash, so tons of junk mail clogs landfills.

Reuse junk mail to create colorful trash-to-treasure paper beads for a necklace.

SUPPLIES

- all of your weekly mail, including junk mail such as catalogs, flyers, and magazine subscription offers
- notepad and pencil
- scale
- fishing line
- ruler
- scissors
- piece of cardboard
- wooden skewer or chopstick
- glue stick
- small brush
- decoupage or Elmer's glue
- metal clasps

Hint: Reuse clasps from broken jewelry. You can also string pearls, beads, and charms along with the completed paper beads.

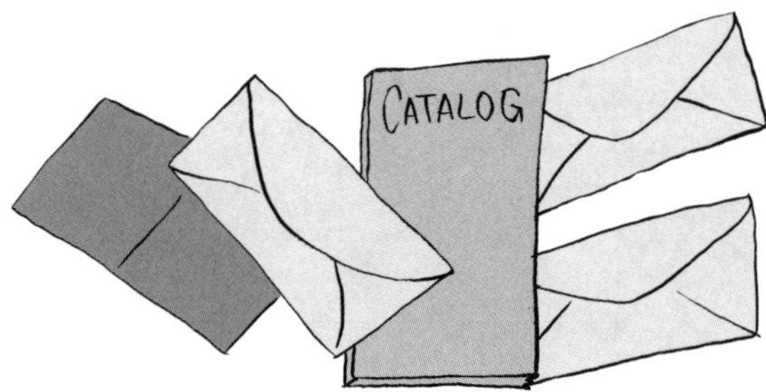

1 Collect all the mail your family receives for one week. Make one pile of regular mail and one of junk mail. Tally the number of pieces in each, and jot down your totals. Weigh each pile and jot down the totals. How do they compare?

2 Place junk mail into categories of your choice. For example, make piles of catalogs, advertisements, or magazine subscription offers. How many pieces are in each pile? Note your findings.

3 Now it's time to reuse your junk mail! First decide how long you'd like your necklace to be. Or maybe you'd like to make a bracelet instead. Measure the length of fishing line you need, and cut it.

4 Create a template with the cardboard. Draw a triangular shape that is 1 inch wide at its base (2½ centimeters) and 6 inches long (15 centimeters). Cut out the template, and use it to trace about 30 strips on glossy paper from your junk mail. Cut out the strips. If you discover later that you need more beads, then come back to this step to make additional strips.

5 Firmly wrap the wide end of the first strip around the skewer, and roll the strip toward the pointed end. The tighter the paper, the more decorative the bead. When you have about 2 inches of the bead left to roll (5 centimeters), use the glue stick to swipe the remaining length with glue.

6 Finish rolling the bead, and hold it firmly in place until the glue sets. Carefully remove the bead from the stick and set aside. Repeat with all the strips until you've made all the beads.

7 For strong, durable beads, seal them with a coat of decoupage glue, or Elmer's glue with water added. This makes a nice finish. You might find that it's easier to apply the glue if you place each bead back on the tip of the skewer first. After applying the glue, set each bead aside to dry.

8 Tightly tie one clasp to an end of the fishing line. When the beads are dried and feel firm to the touch, string them on the line. Once the line is completely full, tightly attach the other clasp. Enjoy your junk mail jewelry!

9 Team up with a parent. Remove your names and address from junk mailing lists. To keep junk mail from showing up in your mailing box, go to the website for the Direct Marketing Association, at www.dmachoice.org.

Milk Jug Mr. Bones

"The back bone's connected to the neck bone. The neck bone's connected to the head bone." Have you ever heard the traditional tune "Dry Bones?" In this project you'll reuse plastic milk jugs to connect the bones of your own skeleton! Ask an adult to help you with the Xacto knife.

SUPPLIES

- 12 washed plastic gallon milk jugs
- permanent marker
- Xacto or craft knife
- scissors
- string
- glue gun
- paper punch
- ruler
- optional: glow-in-the-dark paint and brush

Hint: Depending on how you make your cuts, you might use fewer or more jugs. Look at the picture of the finished skeleton for help.

1. Peel or soak off the labels on the milk jugs. Start at the top of the skeleton, with Mr. Bones' skull. Not all gallon milk jugs look the same, so try to find one that has two round grooves on the side opposite the handle. Those hollowed out circles are the skull's eye sockets. Face the handle away from you, and turn the jug upside down.

2. You're ready to make a skull face. Use the marker to draw a skull's nose and wide, toothy grin. Using the Xacto knife, cut out the eyes, nose, and mouth. Then, cut two ¼-inch slits (6½ millimeters) at the top of the skull. Snip a long piece of string. Thread it through the slits and knot it securely so the completed skeleton can dangle from it.

3. Use another jug. Keep it right side up, and turn the handle away from you. Visualize a chest and ribcage. There's an area in the center of the jug that juts out. On each side of it, draw four rib bones. Slice through the plastic and cut out the sections to complete the ribcage.

4 Join the skull and chest with a neck by using the glue gun to attach the spouts of the two jugs. Hold the jugs firmly in place as the glue sets and cools.

5 For shoulders, cut off the handles of two more jugs. Make sure you leave a curved section of plastic at the ends to attach arms later. Punch a hole at the end of each shoulder. Glue the other end of the shoulders at the sides of the chest, with the punched areas facing out.

6 Stand a jug on a flat surface to build the hips. Measure 4½ inches up from the base of the jug (11½ centimeters). Mark with a horizontal line. Along the line, cut completely around the jug. Stand the smaller bottom piece you cut away on the table. In each of its four sections, snip out a half moon shape. Choose two opposite corners, and punch holes in each. Place the hips aside for now.

7 Ready for the waist? Cut out two bottle spouts, making sure you leave a half-inch section of plastic around the bottom of each (1 centimeter). Glue together the spouts' narrow ends. Glue the chest and hips to the dried waist. Hold firmly in place as the glue sets and dries.

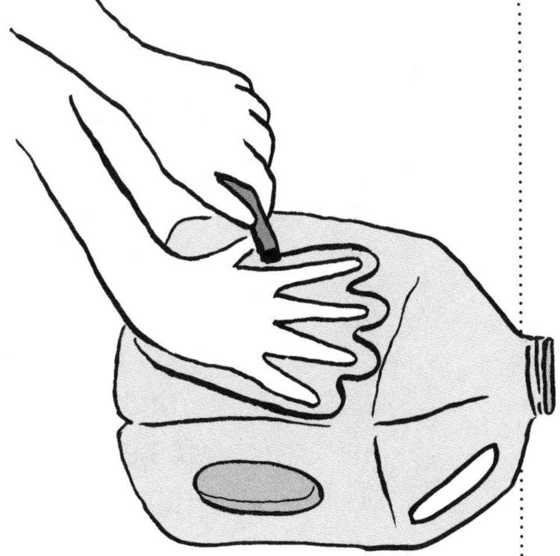

TRY IT!

Using milk jugs, design and build your own decorations. Make kooky masks, scary ghosts, or monsters like Frankenstein.

8 You'll need three jugs to make eight bones for the arms and legs. First, cut into the corner, contoured sections of the jugs to make four bones for the tops of the arms and legs.

continues on next page . . .

9 Now, cut away the center area of the jugs to make the other four bones. They'll become the lower arms and legs. Punch holes through both ends of all the bones. Use string to connect both sets of arm bones. Then tie the arms to the shoulders. Use more string to connect both sets of leg bones. Tie those to the hips.

10 Trace your hands and bare feet on four of the remaining sides of jugs. Cut them out, punch holes where the wrists and ankles will connect to the arms and legs. Tie them to the skeleton.

11 For an eerie touch, coat Mr. Bones with glow-in-the-dark paint. After your skeleton dries, hang him outside and let him rattle his bones in the breeze.

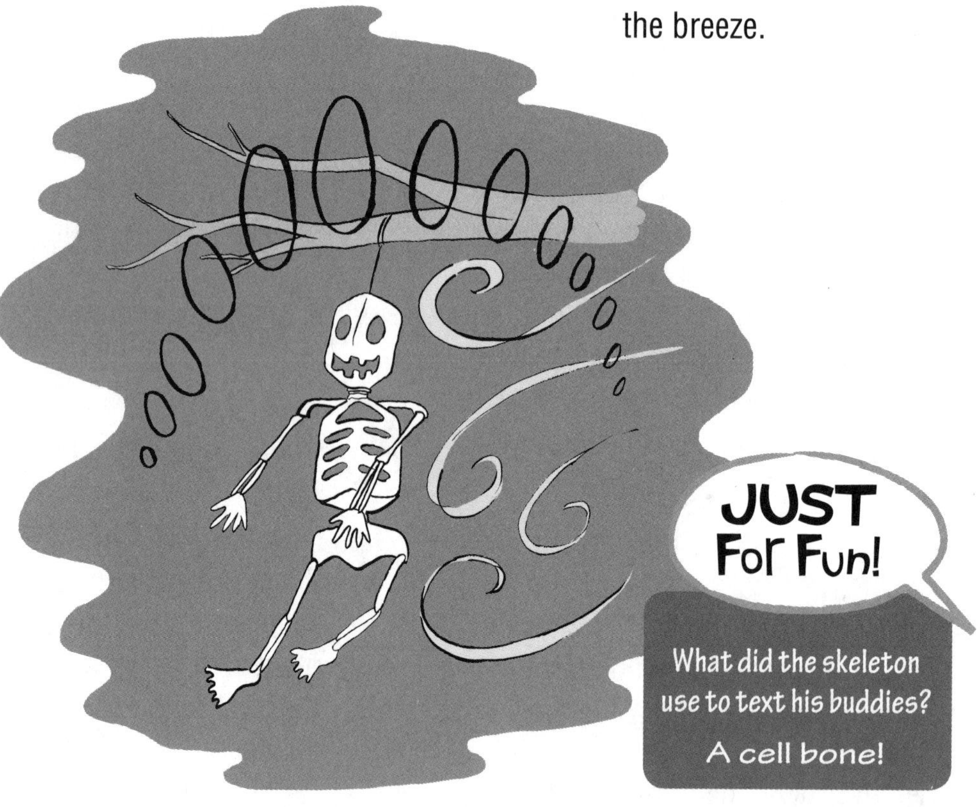

JUST For Fun!

What did the skeleton use to text his buddies?

A cell bone!

Musical Wind Chimes

Do you have spoons that have been mangled in the garbage disposal? Don't chuck them! Reuse them to help make a melodious wind chime. You can later add other items like soda cans or metal pie plates.

SUPPLIES

- drill with a small bit (1/8 inch or 0.3 centimeter)
- 4 old metal spoons
- 1 old fork with four tines
- hammer
- pliers
- scissors
- fishing line
- ruler

1. Ask an adult to drill a hole at the end of each spoon and the fork. Flatten the spoons with a hammer.

2. Use the pliers to bend each of the serving fork's four tines, which are the individual pointy pieces. First, bend the outer tines out to the sides. Then, bend one inner tine backward and the other one forward.

3. Cut a 12-inch piece of fishing line (30 centimeters). Thread one end through one spoon, and securely knot it. Tightly tie the free end to one tine of the serving fork. Repeat with the other spoons. Need an extra set of hands? Ask someone to help you keep the lines from crossing and tangling.

4. Cut a final piece of line, about 22–24 inches long (56–61 centimeters). String it through the hole in the serving fork, and tie a secure loop at the end. Hang your wind chime from a tree

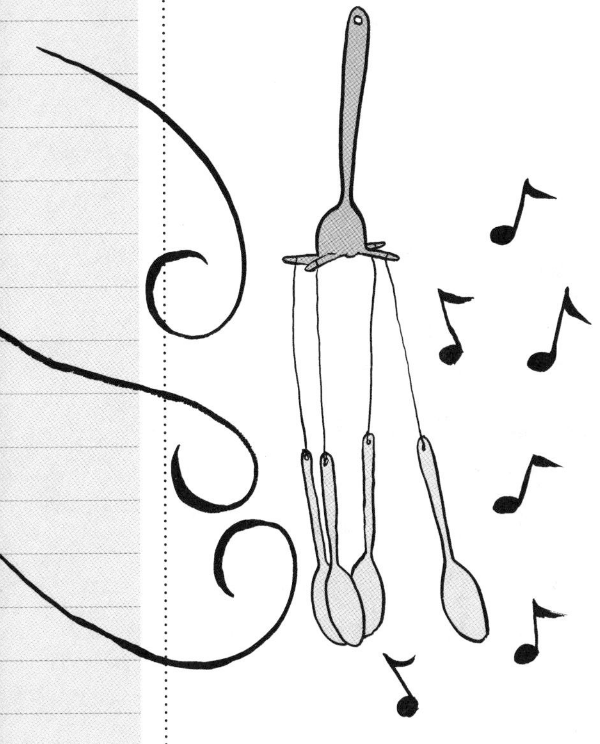

ACTIVITY

CHAPTER 7

Recycle

One of the best ways to prevent items from entering the waste stream is to recycle them. Recycling is a loop, or continuous process. Materials are broken down, then they are built back up again and used to create brand-new objects. Recycling is great because it conserves natural resources, saves energy, and helps the environment.

Materials that can be recycled include plastic, paper, glass, and metal. Recycled materials are used to make more of the same item or to create brand-new products. Your family probably recycles now. To pitch in, separate recyclables from your trash. Bottles, jars, newspapers, junk mail, and even flat tires can be recycled into new products.

Trash Flash

How much trash are you recycling? According to the Clean Air Council, folks in the United States recycle only about one-tenth of their solid garbage. Pitch in to boost that percentage. Not sure which items your community accepts for recycling? Do online research or pop in at your town hall to find out. Notice your family members throwing away recyclables? Take them out of the trash and let your family know what can go in the recycling. Make sure you have recycling bins at home that everyone can get to easily.

Take your recyclables to a recycling center or lug them to the curb, so they can enter the recycling stream. Instead of heading to landfills, recyclables temporarily move to a transfer station or materials recovery plant. At the plant, workers clean, dry, and sort materials before they move along to be **reprocessed**, or broken down.

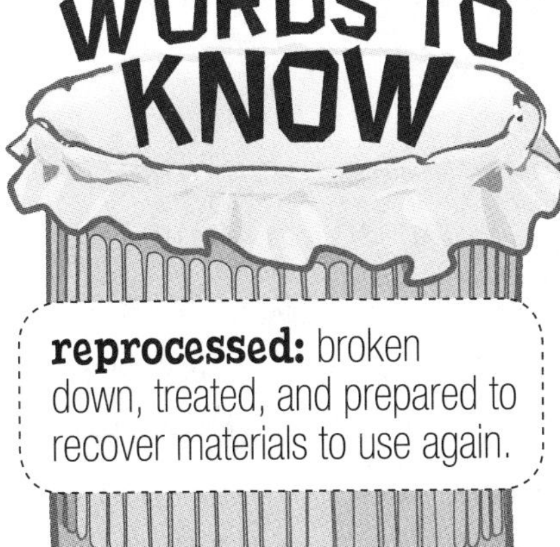

reprocessed: broken down, treated, and prepared to recover materials to use again.

How are materials separated? Mega magnets snatch metals off conveyer belts. Hand sorters stand along the belts and yank out plastics, cardboard, paper, and glass. They separate plastics by identification codes, divide paper into various types, and organize glass according to color.

Trash Flash

Recycling isn't new. Metalworkers from as far back as ancient times melted down gold and silver earrings, rings, and necklaces. Then they used the melted metals to make new jewelry. And whenever there was a new king or emperor, metal crafters got busy. They melted down coins that featured the old ruler and made new coins with the new leaders' profile.

After everything has been separated, it goes to the reprocessing plant. This is where the materials are broken down. Reprocessing plants shred plastics, reduce paper to pulp, crush glass, and melt metals. The broken-down plastic, paper, and glass get tightly bundled into bales. Meanwhile, the melted metal is poured and shaped into bars or blocks. Now these materials are ready to be sold to manufacturers, who use them to produce new items.

When we purchase recyclable and recycled products, we help close the loop.

This means that Earth's natural resources don't get used up. And that means more clean air, soil, and water for the future. So try to read comic books made from newspaper pulp. Buy flip-flops fashioned from shredded plastics. Or string beads crafted from crushed glass.

What Is Recycled?

Materials used to make soft drink, sports drink, and salad dressing bottles can be recycled into new bottles. They can be transformed into entirely new products like fleece clothing, carpeting, and even luggage.

- shampoo bottles, yogurt tubs, and cereal boxes can be recycled into pipes, rope, doghouses, and recycling bins
- blood bags, medical tubing, and window frames can be recycled into new packaging, gutters, mud flaps, and traffic cones
- dry cleaning and frozen food bags, and squeezy mustard bottles can be recycled into compost bins, trashcans, and furniture
- ketchup and medicine bottles, as well as disposable diapers, can be recycled into traffic lights, bike racks, and rakes
- CD cases, egg cartons, and disposable utensils can be recycled into new egg cartons, switch plate covers, and thermometers

TRY IT!

There's a connection between convenience and recycling. Many people really want to recycle—but only if it's not too difficult. Make it easy for others to pitch in. Take a co-mingled recycling bin, which accepts different types of materials, to practices, games, and activities. Urge others to throw in their plastic bottles, cans, and glass instead of lobbing them in to trashcans.

Source: Society of the Plastics Industry, Inc.

Trash Flash

Upcycling is using materials to turn them into something new and better. **Downcycling** is the opposite. Downcyling is recycling materials into new items of lesser quality. Although recycling is a loop, not all materials can go around and around endlessly. Especially paper and plastics. After repeated reprocessing, these materials become too broken down to use. Fresh materials must be added to make them usable again.

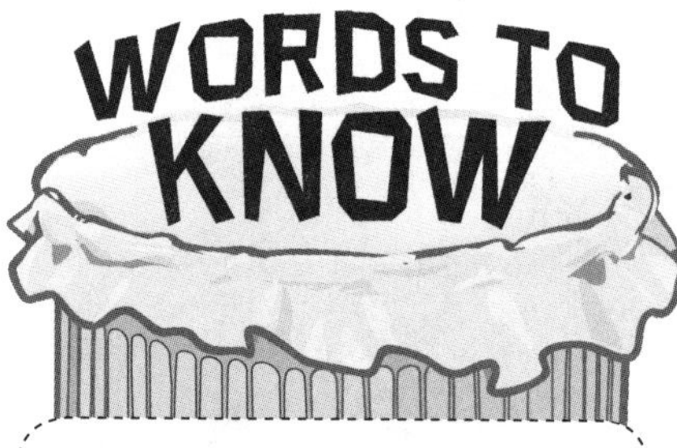

downcycling: recycling materials into something of lesser quality.

e-waste: discarded electronic devices.

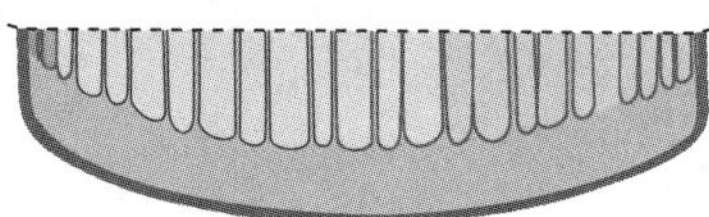

E-Waste

How many electronic gadgets and gizmos do you have? The average American household uses 25! These include smart phones, audio equipment, laptops, game systems, and TVs. And we're constantly upgrading as trendier models come onto the market.

Isn't it annoying when electronics go kaput a few days after the warranty expires? Or the latest gizmo crashes your old system? Blame it on something called "planned obsolescence." This means that products are designed to break down after a certain amount of time. Why? So we'll have to buy new ones! This might be good for business, but it's bad for the environment. According to the United Nations Environmental Program, people around the world trash over 50 million tons (45 million metric tons) of electronic devices every year!

E-waste, or electronic waste, is the fastest-growing category of waste in the United States. E-waste is hazardous because it contains arsenic, lead, and mercury. And you know what happens when hazardous waste gets squished into landfills. It becomes part of the garbage soup that can leak through and contaminate our groundwater and soil.

To prevent this from happening, many communities provide ways to recycle this waste. E-waste recovery centers take apart electronics. They keep bits of copper wire, gold, and platinum that can be used again.

Many people don't know that a lot of our e-waste ends up in countries without strict environmental laws.

Some companies ship e-waste away. They launch it out of sight and out of mind. But it goes somewhere. For example, some of our old computers and cell phones end up in dumps in places like India and Ghana. People rummage through these open dumps and take the electronics apart by hand to scavenge for valuable materials to sell. In the process, they expose themselves to the hazardous materials inside. In China, people burn e-waste in open pits. This contaminates the air, soil, and water. Kids play in toxic ash and develop lead poisoning.

Right now, the United States does not have rules for handling e-waste. So what can you do? One solution is to research the way your community handles e-waste recycling.

Try to find a certified recycling center near you by visiting eStewards at http://e-stewards.org/find-a-recycler/.

Rubbish Warriors

The good ship Plastiki isn't your run-of-the-mill catamaran. This sailboat is made of 12,500 reused plastic bottles, a reclaimed aluminum mast and a recycled cloth sail. In 2010, Plastiki sailed 11,000 miles (17,700 kilometers) across the Pacific Ocean.

Among the crew of six was environmentalist David de Rothschild, who led the expedition. He hit the high seas to call attention to the amount of plastic debris that pollutes the earth's oceans. The voyage from San Francisco, California, to Sydney, Australia, took 128 days. Along the way, the 60-foot catamaran (18 meters) navigated around the Great Pacific Garbage Patch, battling storms and violent waters.

TRY IT!

Did you know Greenphone.com pays you to recycle your old cell phone? The company figures out the trade-in value and sends you a check in that amount. The shipping cost is on them, too. The best news? Greenphone passes repurposed phones to people in need and plants a tree for every device recycled.

Gold, silver, and bronze! What do these Olympic medals have to do with e-waste? A lot, actually. A company in Vancouver, Canada, made the 2010 Winter Olympic medals from recovered metals taken from old computer monitors, laptops, and printers.

Recycled Vision

A girl squints at her baby brother's blurry face. A boy struggles in reading class, unable to make out the words in his book. All over the world, people need glasses. Yet, every year in North America, we throw out 4 million pairs of eyeglasses!

Give the gift of sight. Encourage your family and friends to recycle old glasses. You can donate them to the Lions Club in your community. Many Lions Clubs place convenient drop-off boxes in libraries, schools, and eye doctors' offices. Or you can mail eyeglasses in padded envelopes or boxes (try to reuse some packaging) to:

Lions Clubs International Headquarters

Attention: Receiving Department

300 W. 22nd Street

Oak Brook, IL 60523, USA

Recycled Rainbow Crayons

Don't throw out old broken crayon stubs! Everything old is new again when you melt down stubs to create chunky rainbow crayons. Have an adult help you use the oven.

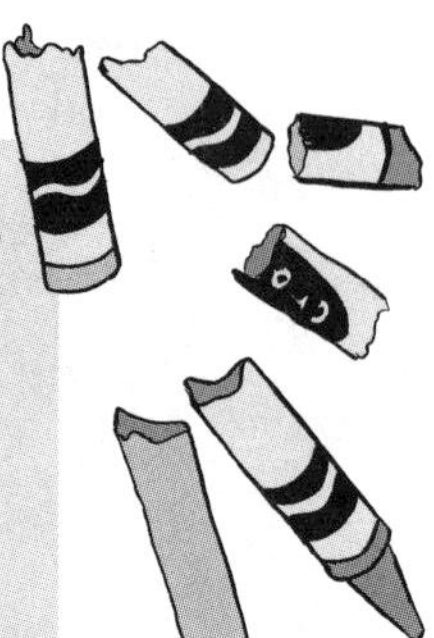

SUPPLIES

- broken crayons or small crayon stubs
- oven
- paper or foil muffin or cupcake liners
- old muffin or cupcake tin

1 Round up stubby and broken crayons, and peel away leftover bits of paper.

2 Preheat the oven to 150 degrees Fahrenheit (65 degrees Celsius). Place the cupcake liners in the muffin tin. Pile the old crayons on top of one another until you fill each liner with a 1-inch layer (2½ centimeters).

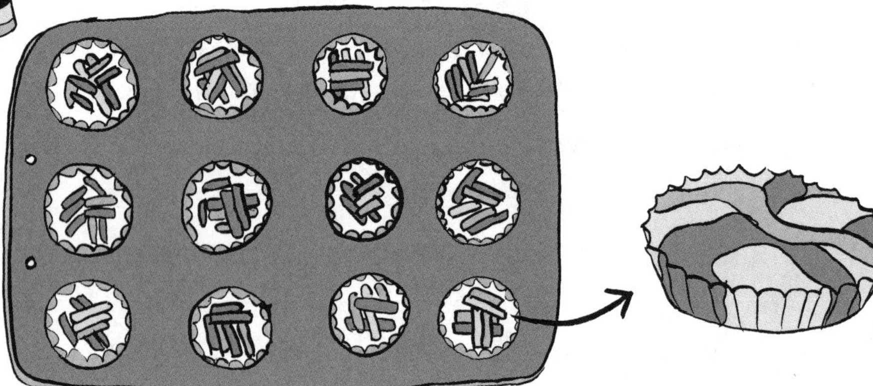

Hint: A sizzling day works for melting crayon stubs, too. Place the stubs on top of liners in the tin. Then leave the tin outside in direct sunlight for about 6 hours.

3 Bake the stubs for 15–20 minutes until fully melted. Remove the tin from the oven, and let the crayons cool for 24 hours. Remove the crayons from the tin and peel away the liners.

ACTIVITY

Fuel for the Fire

Recycle waste paper to create energy and conserve landfill space.

SUPPLIES

- paper products such as cereal boxes, grocery bags, paper cups and plates, napkins and paper towels, and flour and sugar bags
- scissors
- tub of warm water
- cookie sheet
- aluminum foil

HINT: Don't use items that contain wax liners, foams, or plastics.

How do you start a campfire with only two small pieces of wood?

Make sure one is matchstick!

1. Cut the paper products into pieces about 4-inches square (10 centimeters). Place the pieces in the tub of warm water and thoroughly soak them until they become mushy to the touch. Pour out the water.
2. Line the cookie sheet with aluminum foil. Layer the wet paper squares onto the sheet. Build up layers until they are approximately ¾ inch thick (19 millimeters). Press hard with the heel of your hand to compress the layers and squish out the remaining water. Carefully pour out the water.
3. Place the cookie sheet in a warm place to dry for at least 24 hours. Outside in the sun works best.
4. When the layers have completely dried, lift the entire piece out of the pan. Peel away the aluminum foil. Snap or cut off hunks of dried paper to use when you want to build a fire in a fireplace or while camping. They'll burn like wood.

ACTIVITY

CHAPTER 8

Rethink

Rethinking is reconsidering. It's changing your mind about the way you deal with an issue. Trash has been with us since our nomadic ancestors scouted for food and water. Garbage is part of our lives and always will be. However, we can rethink the way we deal with the waste in our lives.

First, think about how you produce garbage in the first place. Then find ways to reduce the amount you need to throw out. You can do this by making wise choices about what you buy. Try to purchase only what you actually need. Then use up everything you buy.

During World War II, the nation united in a common goal. Remember that rhyme? "Use it up, wear it out, make it do, or do without." People joined together to cut down on their use of resources. Imagine what would happen if everyone pitched in to reduce rubbish and change our throwaway world.

You might not see it, but garbage goes somewhere after you toss it out. By the time you doze off tonight, another jam-packed landfill will close. Encourage your friends and family to keep their trash out of landfills. The great news is that there are lots of sustainable ways to go about it. Team up with worms and decomposers to compost organic wastes. Use your creativity to repurpose your old possessions. Recycle everything you can and buy recycled products.

The choices you make each day really do matter. They make a difference right now and for the future.

The earth shares its resources with you. Making sustainable choices lets you give something back to the planet that keeps you alive.

So get the word out. Share with others what you know about garbage and encourage them to help. Every little effort adds up to big changes. As the World Wildlife Fund reminds us, "We need to change the way we live, work, and play. Today." And don't forget Jack, the student who wrote to the Ocean Conservancy. He put it to us simply: "You guys have to step up . . ."

Step up. Make a difference.

Change starts with you.

You're are the earth's future.

Rubbish Warriors

Amelia and Michael Howard shared a dream and were determined to make it come true. The Howards lived on Chicago's South Side, right across the street from a huge vacant lot. Years earlier the lot had been a stockyard, where meatpacking companies slaughtered animals. After the stockyards closed in the 1970s, the vacant lot became a hazardous eyesore. Businesses and construction crews ditched contaminated rubble there, creating an open toxic dump. People were exposed to high levels of lead. It wasn't safe for kids to play there.

TRY IT!

You've met rubbish warriors who are making a difference. What can you do to help the environment?

The Howards rallied their community. Soon all the neighbors shared the Howard's dream: Turn trash into treasure!

Michael Howard rented a bulldozer and with the help of others cleared away 200 tons of waste (181 metric tons). Kids piled up bricks and picked up junk. They planted a large community garden.

Soon eggplant, beans, and tomatoes sprouted. Teens built a gazebo so visitors could enjoy nature in the city. Volunteers even designed a wetland pond with ducks!

Today, Eden Place Nature Center is an urban oasis for all to enjoy. The center raises chickens and sells organic eggs at the farmer's market. It hosts a popular yearly pumpkin festival. What's next? Eden Place plans to reuse a junked school bus to build a solar-powered movie theatre.

And it all started with a dream.

Windowsill Herb Garden

Growing your own food is a fantastic way to conserve energy and resources. For one thing, you won't need fossil fuels for transportation. And there's no packaging involved. In this project, learn to grow what you need and eat what you grow with your own indoor herb garden!

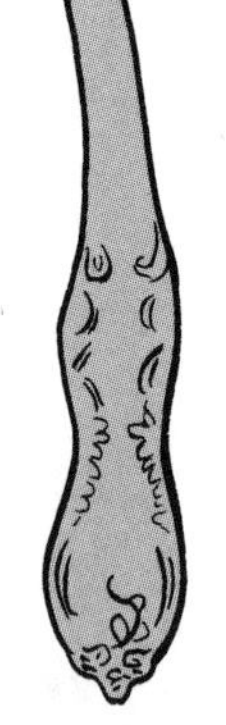

Hint: How does your garden grow? As you tend your plants, notice when they need to be transplanted into larger pots.

SUPPLIES

- 4 old spoons
- scraps of wallpaper or sturdy giftwrap
- colored permanent markers
- scissors
- glue
- 4, 6-inch pots (15 centimeters)
- compost or potting soil
- herb seeds: basil, oregano, dwarf lavender, mint

1 Use spoons and scraps of colorful wallpaper or giftwrap to make decorative labels for your plants. Glue one scrap to the inside of each spoon, and set the spoons aside.

2 Fill each container with potting soil or compost. Read the directions on the seed packets to learn the planting depth for each type of seed. Sprinkle four individual seeds in the center of each pot, according to the recommended depth. As you plant each group of seeds, stick its marker into the back of the pot.

3 Water, but don't drown, each plant. The top of the soil should look wet and feel moist to the touch.

4 Place your herb garden on a flat, stable surface in a warm location that receives plenty of sunshine. Herbs will thrive with 6–8 hours of sun a day.

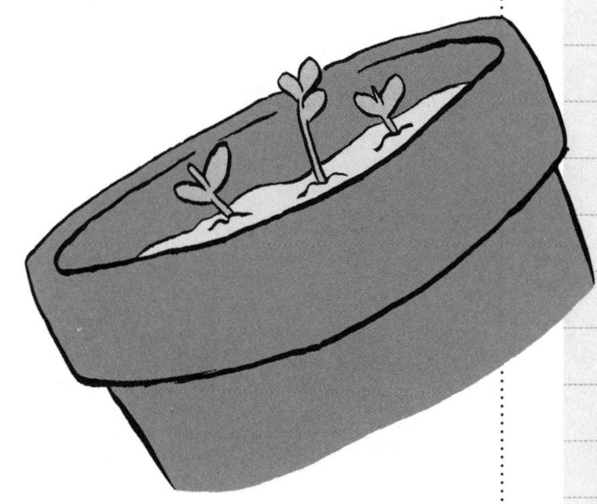

5 When temperatures drop below freezing, move your garden away from window. Keep the pots out of the draft, but try to make sure they still receive sunlight.

6 Depending on the plant, you should see sprouts within three weeks. Allow the surface soil to become dry to the touch between waterings. When the herbs are fully grown, pinch or snip off bits as needed. Add fragrant basil and oregano to pizza, pasta sauces, and soups. Brew soothing mint tea, and dry out lavender for a sweet-smelling potpourri.

What grows between your nose and chin?

Tulips!

ACTIVITY

Fragrant Herbal Shampoo

Check out the list of ingredients on your shampoo bottle. Recognize anything? You probably see a lot of long, complicated names like **sodium laureth sulfate**, **cinnamidopropyltrimonium chloride**, and **cocamidopropyl betaine**. If you don't like the idea of putting these chemicals in your hair, make homemade shampoo using herbs from your indoor garden! Have an adult help you boil the water.

sodium laureth sulfate: a detergent used in shampoos to make it lather up.

cinnamidopropyltrimonium chloride: a sunscreen used in shampoos.

cocamidopropyl betaine: a detergent used in shampoos to make it thicker.

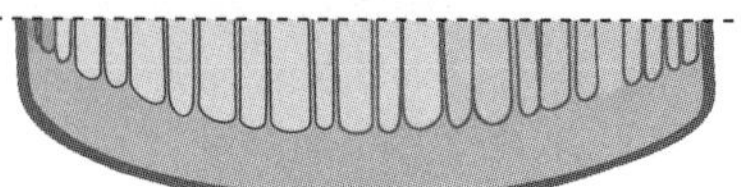

1. Crush dried lavender flowers with the rolling pin until you have 4 tablespoons. With your hands, shred the mint leaves into tiny pieces, and measure 4 tablespoons. Place the herbs into the mixing bowl.

2. Pour the distilled water into the pot, and bring it to a vigorous boil. Remove the pot from the burner, and pour the water over the herbs. Let the herbs soak for 20–30 minutes. Check after 20 minutes to see if the scent is strong enough for you. If not, let it sit for 10 more minutes.

Hint: Do you have light hair? Beware! This recipe could stain your locks with dark color. Replace lavender flowers and mint leaves with dried chamomile and dried yellow marigolds.

SUPPLIES

- 4 tablespoons dried lavender flowers
- rolling pin
- 4 tablespoons fresh mint leaves
- measuring spoon
- mixing bowl
- 7 ounces distilled water (200 milliliters)
- pot
- stove
- 4 tablespoons liquid Castille soap
- 8-ounce shampoo container (plastic or glass) with cap to reuse (230 milliliters)
- strainer

3 In the meantime, pour the Castille soap into the shampoo container. Then check on your herbs again. When they're ready, strain the herb water so that only the liquid remains. Pour it into the shampoo container, and tightly cap it. Shake the shampoo to blend the ingredients. Make sure it's thoroughly cool before use.

What did Ghost Girl wash her hair with?

Shamboo!

TRY IT!

Experiment with natural hair conditioners. For example, after you shampoo, massage 2 tablespoons of plain, fresh yogurt into your hair. Wait a few minutes, then rinse.

ACTIVITY

Organize a No-Waste Lunch

Stop lunch trash! Encourage your school to pitch in—instead of pitching trash out—to make a difference. Challenge everyone to participate in a no-waste lunch.

1. Team up with a group of friends. Speak to your teachers and principal about your plans and arrange a date for the no-waste lunch.
2. Make posters and fliers to get the word out. Include a clever slogan and an eye-catching design. Incorporate information about items that produce waste and those that don't. Publicize the date on your class or school website and during daily announcements. Encourage everyone in your school community to participate.
3. After the no-waste lunch, have a debriefing session. How did things go? What changes will you make for next time? How can you make waste-free lunches a common practice?

JUST For Fun!

What do you call shoes made from banana peels?

Slippers!

Waste	No-Waste
• plastic grocery bag or single-serving lunch kit	• lunch box, bento box, reusable bag
• plastic water bottle, beverage can, juice bag, juice box, mini milk carton, straw	• stainless steel water bottle, thermos
• paper napkins	• cloth napkins
• plastic utensils	• silverware from home
• single-serving bag of pretzels	• pretzels in a reusable container
• single-serving fruit in a plastic package	• apple, banana, orange, peach, or other fruit, cut up in a reusable container
• sandwich wrapped in plastic, foil, or wax paper	• sandwich packed in a reusable container

ACTIVITY

Rubbish Warriors

Back when Mackenzie Cowles was in fifth grade at Greenbrook Elementary School in Danville, California, her class tracked and weighed the garbage dumped in the cafeteria. Mackenzies's classmates couldn't believe what kids threw out—full juice boxes, unopened bags of chips, whole bananas, oranges, and apples. Even ice packs!

Mackenzie's classmates challenged the entire school to reduce their waste and help the environment. They designed posters and held a no-waste lunch. Her class even created a Share Basket. If someone didn't eat a banana, for example, he or she placed it in the Share Basket. If kids forgot to bring lunch or felt extra hungry, they could grab something out of the basket.

JUST For Fun!

What did one plate say to the other?

Hey, lunch is on me!

Years later, Mackenzie recalls how the project changed her actions. "Now, when I eat or drink, I take only the amount I can finish," she explained. "If there's something left in my lunch, I don't throw it away. I save it in my backpack and eat it for a snack later. It's really important to help the planet. Good things come back."

GOOD THINGS COME BACK!

archaeologist: a scientist who studies past human life.

artifact: an object made by people from past cultures, including tools, pottery, and jewelry.

biodegradable: able to decay and break down.

biodegradation: the process of materials naturally breaking down.

capacity: the maximum amount something can hold.

catastrophic: involving or causing large amounts of damage.

cell: a storage space for garbage in a landfill.

chamber pot: a jug or bowl stashed under beds as a personal port-a-potty.

cinnamidopropyltrimonium chloride: a sunscreen used in shampoos.

closed-loop life cycle: the life cycle for organic material that never comes to an end.

cocamidopropyl betaine: a detergent used in shampoos to make it thicker.

compactor: a machine that tightly packs trash.

compostable: a material that can break down and rot in a compost heap.

compost: decayed food scraps and vegetation that can be put back in the soil.

compress: to squeeze and squish things to make them smaller.

contaminant: a poisonous or polluting substance.

data: information, facts, and numbers.

decay: to rot

decomposers: bacteria, insects, and fungi that break down plant and animal wastes and cause them to decay.

delirious: restlessness, confusion, and excitement brought on by a high fever, often with mixed-up speech.

dioxin: an extremely toxic chemical that can be released from burning some materials.

disposable: made to be thrown away after using once.

downcycling: recycling materials into something of lesser quality.

Environmental Protection Agency (EPA): a department of the government concerned with the environment and its impact on human health.

environment: everything in nature, living and nonliving, including animals, plants, rocks, soil, and water.

epidemic: a disease that hits large groups at the same time and spreads quickly.

e-waste: discarded electronic devices.

excavate: to dig out a site and its artifacts for study.

exhaust: use up.

flammable: easily set on fire.

fossil fuels: oil, coal, or gas that formed in the earth from decayed plants or animals.

fungi: mold, mildew, rust, and mushrooms. Plural of fungus.

garbologist: an archaeologist who studies garbage.

greenhouse gas: a gas such as water vapor, carbon dioxide, and methane that traps heat and contributes to warming temperatures.

groundwater: underground water supplies.

hazardous waste: chemical or toxic materials such as pesticides and paint thinners that hurt people, animals, and the environment.

incinerator: a large furnace that burns trash.

industrialized: when there is a lot of manufacturing. Products are made by machines in large factories.

infectious: able to spread quickly from one person to others.

inorganic: not part of the living world, such as tin and glass.

landfill: a huge area of land where trash gets buried.

leachate: liquid produced in landfills as garbage decays.

linear life cycle: the life cycle for inorganic material that comes to an end when it is thrown away.

manufactured: made by machines.

medical waste: waste generated at hospitals and doctor's offices, such as needles, bandages, or blood.

methane: a greenhouse gas produced by rotting garbage.

midden: an ancient garbage heap.

monitor: to watch, keep track of, or check.

nomadic: moving from place to place to find food.

nutrients: the substances in food and soil that keep animals and plants healthy and growing.

organic: something that is or was living, such as wood, paper, grass, and insects.

pesticides: chemicals used to kill pests like rodents or insects.

possessions: things you own.

precycling: buying less and creating less waste.

preventive: stopping something before it happens.

processed food: food that has added ingredients to make it look nicer, taste better, last longer, or cost less.

ration: limiting the amount of somthing to be used each week or month.

recycle: shredding, squashing, pulping, or melting items to use the materials to create new products.

reduce: to use less of something.

renewable: something that can be replaced after we use it.

reprocessed: broken down, treated, and prepared to recover materials to use again.

repurpose: to change an item and use it for a new purpose.

resource: things found in nature. such as wood or gold, that people can use.

resourceful: able to think of creative solutions to problems.

rethink: to reconsider—to think about something again and change your mind about it.

reuse: instead of tossing out an item, using it again or for a new or creative purpose.

runoff: produced when water picks up wastes as it flows over the surface of the ground. Runoff can pollute streams, lakes, rivers, and oceans.

rupture: to burst or break suddenly.

salvaged: recovered parts or materials that were recycled or reused.

sanitation worker: a person hired to collect and dispose of garbage.

scavenge: to find usable bits and parts from discarded stuff.

sewage: waste from buildings, carried away through sewers. A sewer is a drain for waste.

slaughterhouse: a place where animals are killed for food.

slops: a mushy mixture of kitchen scraps and liquid fed to pigs.

sludge: oozy waste materials in sewage.

sodium laureth sulfate: a detergent used in shampoos to make it lather up.

source reduction: reducing the quantity of waste, especially in packaging, so there is less to dispose of.

statistics: numbers that show facts about a subject.

suburb: where people live near a city.

sustainability: living in a way that uses resources wisely, so they don't run out.

technology: tools, methods, and systems used to solve a problem or do work.

thrift: using money carefully.

toxic: poisonous.

upcycle: to remake old products into something more environmentally friendly, and often of better quality and value.

vermicomposting: using worms in composting to break down and recycle food wastes.

vermin: small animals or insects that are pests, like cockroaches or mice.

waste stream: the flow of household and industrial garbage that gets hauled away, recycled, incinerated, or disposed of in landfills.

RESOURCES

Books, Media, and Web sites

- Cantor, Norman. ***In the Wake of the Plague: The Black Death and the World It Made.*** The Free Press, 2001.
- Grossman, Elizabeth. ***High Tech Trash: Digital Devices, Hidden Toxics, and Human Health.*** Island Press, 2006.
- Kelly, John. ***Great Mortality: An Intimate History of the Black Death.*** Fourth Estate Limited, 2005.
- Murphy, Jim. ***An American Plague: The True and Terrifying Story of the Yellow Fever Epidemic of 1793.*** Clarion Books, 2003.
- Rathji, William and Cullen Murphy. ***Rubbish! The Archaeology of Garbage.*** University of Arizona Press, 2001.
- Rockliff, Mara. ***Get Real: What Kind of World Are You Buying?*** Running Press, 2010.
- Rogers, Helen. ***Gone Tomorrow: The Hidden Life of Trash.*** The New Press, 2001.
- Royte, Elizabeth. ***Bottlemania: How Water Went on Sale and Why We Bought It.*** Bloomsbury USA, 2008.
- Royte, Elizabeth. ***Garbage Land: On the Secret Trail of Trash.*** Back Bay Books, 2006.
- Shoup, Kate. ***Rubbish! Reuse Your Refuse.*** Wiley Publishing, 2008.
- Strasser, Susan. ***Waste and Want: A Social History of Trash.*** Metropolitan Books/Henry Holt, 1999.
- Streissguth, Thomas, ed. ***The Black Death.*** Greenhaven Press, 2004.
- CBS News. ***60 Minutes: The Electronic Wasteland, produced by Solly Granatstein.*** November 10, 2008.

- CNBC Television. ***Trash Inc: The Secret Life of Garbage.*** Produced by Mitch Weitzner, Wally Griffith, and Alison O'Brien. September 29, 2010.
- http://www.astc.org/exhibitions/rotten/rthome.htm ***Rotten Truth About Garbage***
- http://storyofstuff.org/bottledwater/ ***The Story of Bottled Water***, Susan Leonard
- http://www.storyofstuff.com/ ***The Story of Stuff Project***, Susan Leonard
- http://wwf.panda.org/about_our_earth/all_publications/living_planet_report/2010_lpr/ ***WWF, Living Planet Report***, 2010

Explore These Web sites

- http://www.greatlakes.org/Page.aspx?pid=525
  Alliance for the Great Lakes, Adopt-a-Beach
- http://www.cleanair.org/Waste/wasteFacts.html
  Clean Air Council, Waste Reduction and Recycling Program
- http://www.kidsecologycorps.org/forkids.html ***EPA Environmental Kids Clu***b
- http://www.epa.gov/osw/education/pdfs/sciencefair.pdf ***EPA Science Fair Fun***
- http://dnr.wi.gov/org/caer/ce/eek/earth/recycle/
  EEK! Environmental Education for Kids, Recycling
- http://ecoguru.panda.org/ ***Eco Guru: Measure your ecological footprint, and discover the positive impact of your changes***
- http://kids.niehs.nih.gov/recycle.htm ***National Institute of Environmental Sciences Kids' Pages: Reduce, Reuse, and Recycle***
- www.oceanconservancy.org ***Ocean Conservancy***
- http://www.riverkeeper.org ***Riverkeeper***
- http://www.wastefreelunches.org/ ***Waste Free Lunches***
- http://library.oregonmetro.gov/files//green_cleaners.pdf
  Find more fabulous green cleaner recipes at Oregon Metro
- http://oceanservice.noaa.gov/education/for_fun/EndangeredSpeciesOrigami.pdf
  Follow directions to make junk mail origami sea turtles and whales

A

B

C

D

E

F

G

R

S

T

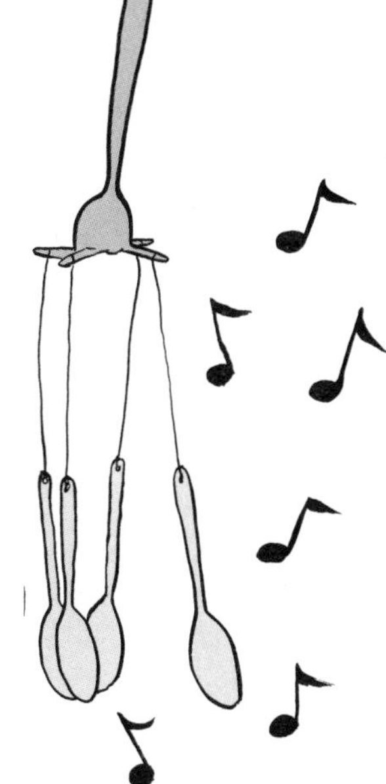

U

V

W

Y